D0067076

TSUNAMI
of the Spirit:
Come Roll Over Me

A Festschrift *for*
General Paul &
Commissioner
Kay Rader

EDITED BY JOE NOLAND & STEPHEN COURT

CREST BOOKS

Salvation Army National Headquarters
Alexandria, VA, USA

Copyright © 2014 by The Salvation Army

Published by Crest Books
The Salvation Army National Headquarters
615 Slaters Lane
Alexandria, VA 22313
Phone: 703/684-5523

Major Allen Satterlee, Editor in Chief and National Literary
Secretary
Roger Selvage, Cover Design
Judith L. Brown, Crest Books Editor

Available from The Salvation Army Supplies and Purchasing
Departments
      Des Plaines, IL – (847) 937-8896
      West Nyack, NY – (888) 488-4882
      Atlanta, GA – (800) 786-7372
      Long Beach, CA – (847) 937-8896

Also visit www.shop.salvationarmy.org

Printed in the United States of America

All rights reserved. No part of this publication may be reproduced,
stored in a retrieval system, or transmitted in any form or by any
means without prior written permission of the publisher. Exceptions
are brief quotations in printed reviews.

ISBN: 978-0-9913439-1-1

Library of Congress Control Number: 2014933735

Dedication

A festschrift is a collection of writings published in honor of someone. This festschrift celebrates General Paul and Commissioner Kay Rader on the occasion of his 80th birthday.

The classic dedication as it appears on Salvation Army cornerstones around the world honors the Raders to the glory of God and the salvation of the world.

Contents

Foreword

When we look at our history, particularly the early days, the Army readily adopted unorthodox and innovative ideas. In looking at the Army now, however, could the same be said of our generation today? We do seem to see many people with a maintenance mentality. In too many places around the world we have generations of Salvationists who have only experienced decline. Other churches used to adopt some of our methods, but today we see places where we appear content to copy from other churches.

Generally speaking we are creatures of habit and enjoy the comfort of routine. Someone reputedly said: "If Christians had been present with God at creation, the chances are they would have voted for the status quo — chaos!" The world is in constant flux with change taking place at tremendous speed. We have seen this in our lifetime, and the pace of change is a huge challenge — to politicians, to business, but also to the Church.

Change is generally resisted and we have seen increasing signs of resistance, at times even violent opposition, to some of the economic and political changes that were deemed necessary in recent years. We see a similar phenomenon in the Church where people resist sometimes the smallest of changes on the basis that "we've always done it this way" or "this is Army!"

Army leaders are not sheltered from the pain that change management brings. One of the challenges for us is to find ways to create space for people to be able to contribute, to create and innovate. Old ways of doing things are not necessarily right for today, and probably less so for tomorrow.

André Cox was the 24th Chief of the Staff and is the 20th General of The Salvation Army, currently leading a movement active in 126 countries. He is the first African-born General, having served in Zimbabwe, Switzerland, Finland, South Africa, and England. Like his father, he also served as the Chief of the Staff.

It is said that "doing the same thing over and over, yet expecting different results is the definition of insanity," while Roger von Oech observed: "It's easy to come up with new ideas; the hard part is letting go of what worked for you two years ago, but will soon be out of date." There are some in the world today who wish that time had stopped and they could live back in an era when things seemed more secure. When faced with change, it is easy to wish that things would remain as they were to avoid facing upheaval or new challenges.

As Christians, we should not only look back at the past but be forward looking as well. After all, we believe in a bright future. Do we not? The prophet Isaiah reminds us of a great spiritual truth when he says: "...but those who hope in the LORD will renew their strength. They will soar on wings like eagles; they will run and not grow weary, they will walk and not be faint." (Isaiah 40:31)

"Looking Forward" reflects a life and leadership characteristic of General Paul A. Rader (Ret.) and Commissioner Kay Rader. It is our prayer that we too will experience that reality as we go forward into the future with God.

André Cox, General
London

Introduction

Shortly after his election to General, Paul Rader issued a call to prayer and mission. Within that clarion call was this rallying cry: "Pray that a Spirit-inspired movement of prayer reaching the throne of God will bring a mighty tidal wave of salvation blessing sweeping over our army around the world, a tsunami of the spirit, cleansing, refreshing and renewing us for mission."

It's appropriate and timely that his use of the metaphor, "tsunami of the spirit," be selected as the title for this festschrift. Experts have identified four stages of tsunami formation, and they are presented herein, as a spiritual extension of this metaphorical comparison.

The Initiation Stage (Creation and Motion)

Something occurs, usually an earthquake on the ocean floor, creating kinetic energy (setting into motion) the beginnings of a giant wave. It is the energy created in a body of water because of its motion.

"In the beginning, God created..." setting into motion a redemptive tidal wave, ebbing and flowing as the battle between good and evil raged on (Creation and Motion). Consider the ebb and flow throughout the Old and New Testaments, where new beginnings resulted in redemptive tidal waves (Creation and Motion). In a new beginning, with William and Catherine as His holy instruments, God created... In a new beginning, with Paul and Kay as His holy instruments, God created... In God's perfect timing, four examples out of many, chosen and called to initiate a new beginning, a tsunami of the spirit.

"God is calling our Army to prayer! ...in mission" Rader (Creation and Motion)

The Splitting Stage (Crisis and Opportunity)

Here, the wave splits, traveling in opposing directions, resulting in a swirling of chaos and crisis. Opportunity always emerges out of crisis.

In every salvation experience, there is always a crisis moment.
Saul (Crisis) Paul (Salvation)
Submerged Tenth (Crisis) The Salvation Army (Salvation).
20th Century Decadence (Crisis) 21st Century Revival (Salvation).
"The salvation war in which we are engaged is real." Rader (Crisis and Opportunity)

The Amplification Stage (Risk and Possibility)

The amplitude increases, resulting in a steepening of the wave. The steeper the wave, the more powerful and dangerous it becomes, a power that can be channeled for evil or for good, depending upon the final outcome.

Danger is no stranger to Christianity, riskiness a prelude to possibility. Peter's martyrdom opened the floodgates of Christianity, spreading quickly, globally. Martin Luther's daring "95 Theses" ignited a worldwide reformation. The courage of early day Army pioneers defied a Skeleton Army, et al., the enemy defeated as Salvationist ranks exploded exponentially. And so the amplification ebb and flow continues, as it marches dangerously into the 21st century.

"The enemy against whom we fight is powerful." Rader (Risk and Possibility)

The Run Up Stage (Salvationism and Mission)

A rapid, local rise in sea level as the wave runs up on shore, bringing cleansing in some instances, and destruction in others.

A Tsunami (Run Up) of the Spirit brings destruction to the enemy, and a cleansing to its converts, "a mighty tidal wave of salvation... cleansing, refreshing and renewing us for mission."

"But he (the enemy) is not invincible." Rader (Salvationism and Mission)

The *Four Stages of a Spiritual Tsunami* represents the structure for all that will follow, including the full context of then General Paul Rader's...

A call to prayer and mission

GOD is calling our Army to prayer! He is calling us to urgent, prevailing prayer for the renewal of our love for Christ, a recommitment to our spiritual priorities in mission, and a clearer vision of his purpose for the Army as we approach the year 2000.

The salvation war in which we are engaged is real. The enemy against whom we fight is powerful. But he is not invincible. Indeed, he was defeated at the Cross and exposed to open shame (Colossians 2:15). Still, the battle rages on. Never has the conflict been more intense. Never has there been a greater need for prayer.

We rejoice in every evidence of a revival of prayer in our ranks and beyond — prayer fellowship, prayer vigils, prayer marches, prayer support teams for musical sections, schools of prayer, nights of prayer, concerts of prayer and much more. In 100 countries around our globe the voices of Salvationists in prayer ascend to the throne of grace every hour, day and night. We are a praying Army. But let us confess that for all too many of us, prayer may quickly become a lifeless routine, an empty and powerless ritual, if it is not neglected altogether.

Let every Salvationist take a personal inventory of the place, priority and power of prayer in his or her own life. Do I have a regular time for personal and family worship and prayer? What is the place of prayer in our planning and programs at our corps and centers? When do we pray? Who prays? With what expectation? With what result? Is God calling some of us to a specific ministry of intercession or spiritual warfare through prayer?

As General of The Salvation Army, I am asking that every Salvationist and every center of Army activity consider making a specific commitment to prayer for the next 12 months. The nature of that commitment should be negotiated personally with the Holy Spirit. I seek a commitment beyond our present routines. Let prayer be more disciplined, more specific, more consistent.

For what, then, shall we pray?

• Pray for peace and an end to tribal and ethnic violence, while confessing our own failure to be instruments of His peace. Ask God where we ourselves might bring healing as His ambassadors of reconciliation (2 Corinthians 5:18-20) — in our homes, our marriages, our corps, and our communities.

- Pray for unity among us, the two or three together in his name, and as a global force for salvation and healing of the nations — partners in mission.

- Pray for the salvation of the lost — for a new spirit of holy aggression in our evangelism.

- Pray for world evangelization — the salvation of the unreached peoples of earth, according to "the command of the eternal God, so that all nations might believe and obey him" (Romans 16:26 NIV 1984).

- Pray for the growth of the Army in spiritual depth and devotion. Pray for new corps and new people, "brought out of the dominion of darkness and into the kingdom of the Son he loves" (General Rader, based on Colossians 1:13).

- Pray that God will raise up an Army of senior soldiers, women and men, a million strong, around the world, marching under the one flag.

- Pray for Army leaders — for vision, grace and courage. Pray for them not just as leaders, but also as vulnerable human persons.

- Pray for the confusion and defeat of all the stratagems of Satan and for the deliverance of those held captive to his will.

- Pray for the salvation and moral protection of our young people, for a love for the Word of God, courage to stand for Christ, and a willingness to give radical obedience to His will.

- Pray for officer candidates, lay volunteers, and those who in midlife will put their skills and experience at God's disposal.

- Pray for our Army's worldwide ministries of helping, healing and wholeness among the sick, the powerless, and the poorest of the poor.

- Pray for children caught in the crossfire of war, the homeless, brutalized and abandoned.

- Pray for the beauty of the Lord our God to be upon us as a movement — the beauty of His holiness (Psalm 90:17).

- Pray for a new appreciation of our royal privilege of coming to God at his invitation, for a daily audience with our Savior King, "that we may receive mercy and find grace to help us in our time of need" (Hebrews 4:16).

- Pray that a Spirit-inspired movement of prayer reaching the throne of God will bring a mighty tidal wave of salvation blessing sweeping over our Army around the world, a tsunami of the spirit, cleansing, refreshing and renewing us for mission.

- Pray that Jesus Christ will be glorified through this His Army.

On our knees, let us look again at our own homes, our communities, and our world, careening out of control toward the next century. If you believe with me that God is calling His Army to prayer, then decide now to do something about it — and do it now, for Jesus' sake, and for the salvation of the world for which He died. Let us go forward — on our knees!

General Paul A. Rader
Westminster Central Hall, London, November 1994

The Initiation
(Creation and Motion)

"I think there is always a tendency to settle down in comfort, but our track record here has been to encourage innovation…We want to be on the cutting edge..."

General Paul A. Rader, *Los Angeles Times* interview, July 30, 1994.

O boundless salvation! deep ocean of love,
O fullness of mercy, **Christ brought from above,**
The whole world redeeming, so rich and so free,
Now flowing for all men, now flowing for all men.

Genesis

"Praise to the Lord... the King of Creation"

Joe and Doris Noland

Some see things as they were.
Others see things as they are.
Few see things as they will be.

Something New

Innovate: Introducing, inventing something new or original

Genesis: The origin, source, creation, or coming into being of something

"When God began creating the heavens and the earth, the earth was a shapeless, chaotic mass, with the Spirit of God brooding over the dark vapors" (Genesis 1:1-2 TLB).

Created: baaraa': "create, give being to something new" (Barne's Notes).
"The Enthroned continued,
'Look! I'm making everything new.'"
(Rev. 21:5, The Message)

"Every time we say, 'Let there be!' in any form, something happens"
—Stella Terrill Mann

"Whatever you can do or dream you can, begin it. Boldness has genius, power and magic in it. Begin it now! —Van Goethe

I never use the term, "out-of-the-box thinking" because with God boxes don't exist, nary a one to "think out of."

Joe and Doris Noland, who soldier at The Rock, Waianae, Hawaii, first met the Raders up close and personal during their welcome meeting as territorial leaders in the West, having produced a welcoming segment in the program that evening featuring real Disney characters and a Ronald Reagan lookalike. "Little did we know then, that Disney-like 'imagineering' would be part of their leadership ethos," reflects Joe. "We were given freedom to create and innovate... and it felt so liberating!"

Out-of-the-box thinking is clearly nonsensical,
It's absurd, boring, silly and whimsical
Would God be accused of thinking such?
Alas, He wouldn't have created much.
Boxes non-existent to the All-Seeing,
Boundary free when He brings into being.
No old boxes when creating you:
"Behold! I'm making everything new."

LET THERE BE!

"Yes!" to Genesis

In the beginning God was saying "No!" to status quo (chaos) and "Yes!" to Genesis (Creation): Sky, land, oceans, plants, sun, moon, fish, wild animals, cattle, reptiles, man, woman: Let There Be! Genesis is the spiritual counterpart to innovation (a secularly derived concept). Genesis takes the "no" out of innovation and replaces it with "yes." Allow me to invent a new word here, "Inyesvation" which now becomes a modern Genesis counterpoint.

Culture: "the set of shared attitudes, values, goals, and practices that characterizes an institution or organization" (Merriam-Webster).

Every new innovation will ultimately create its own unique culture, appropriate for that particular time, place and setting. As Genesis continues to unfold, there will be a natural reluctance to embrace and assimilate each new ethos as it emerges, clinging tight to what has now become status quo ("things as they were/are"). Nostalgia is a powerful emotion, none of us immune to it. Thus eventually our "clinging" will be defined by "an unhealthy refusal to let go of the past," diminishing into a new form of chaos. In other words, "the enemy is us."

Chaos is the incubator for creativity and innovation. Genesis occurs when we say "No!" to status quo and "Yes!" to need (things as they will be). Another word for status quo is, "culture."

Cultures collide.
Chaos ensues.
Cravings arise.

Crave: "to have a strong desire for something" (Encarta).
Need-Based Response
Genesis is the creative response to our need-based cravings. John Stott said, "Vision begins with a holy discontent with the way things are." Allow me to substitute the word, "vision," with the word, Genesis, in this context.

Necessity: "The mother of invention" (Plato). This idea is best illustrated in one of Aesop's Fables, "The Crow and the Pitcher."

A crow perishing with thirst saw a pitcher, and hoping to find water, flew to it with delight. When he reached it, he discovered to his grief that it contained so little water that he could not possibly get at it (chaos). He tried everything he could think of to reach the water, but all his efforts were in vain. At last he collected as many stones as he could carry and dropped them one by one with his beak into the pitcher, until he brought the water within his reach and thus saved his life (Genesis).

Creation is always born out of chaos. Evil enters into the equation relapsing into chaos followed by a yearning for re-creation…

Evil, chaos, Genesis…
Evil, chaos, Genesis…
Evil, chaos…

And thus it has been since time began: Serpent ~ Adam; Babel ~ Noah; Sodom ~ Abraham and 42 generations on (Matt. 1:17), God is looking at an empty stage again (shapeless, chaotic mass), totally devoid of a Creative presence (void/chaos).

"He was in the world, the world was there through him, and yet the world didn't even notice" (John 1:9-10).

Devoid of its Soul!

A baby grand piano has always been on my wife's "wish" list. Early on in our ministry, that "wish" was mysteriously granted in the form of a gift to her. She was deliriously ecstatic, rearranging the furniture in preparation for its delivery.

On that eventful day, the movers gingerly placed it in the space arranged as we all gathered around feasting our eyes upon this regal, sparkling white musical instrument. We stood transfixed as she sat down on the bench, lifted the keyboard cover and began to play. Shockingly, as she pressed down on the keys there was no sound. Her fingers danced across the black and white ivories, not one of them so much as emitting a note. We stared at each other dumbfounded.

Upon lifting the lid and peaking inside, NOTHING! Void, shapeless, chaotic! After some further investigative work we found that the piano had been made for a movie prop, an illusion, a husk, devoid of its soul, the very thing that gives it life. And all of this unbeknown to the donor, who upon receiving it, passed it on to us with nary a testing tap on the keys.

Alas, chaos (a state of utter confusion) ensued, crying out for one of those "Something New" Genesis moments. In the garage, we frantically searched for and found our dust-laden portable CD player, popped in a "The Best of Liberace" CD, and then strategically placed it deep within the piano cavity.

Doris sat down at the keyboard. LET THERE BE! I touched the "on" button as she simultaneously touched the ivories and, miracle of miracles, her playing equaled the sound and touch of the master, Liberace. YES!

The Genesis Thinker understands that chaos equals opportunity, and then moves instinctively to creatively fill the void.

Culture and Creation Collide

When Jesus came, culture and Creation collided. This was another of those quintessential Genesis moments. Jesus invaded "the chaos beyond culture" with "antidotes for the stagnation of status quo." Read the Gospels and you will find that He penetrated the chaos with an exclamatory "No!" to status quo, and a resounding "Yes!" to need: You don't have to read far before His clash with the religious culture of the day becomes proactively evident. John gets right to the heart of it quickly: "Stop turning my Father's house into a shopping mall!" – Chief Priests profiting by "filthy lucre," broken and fallen, sinful and diseased (John 2:12-22). Jesus is challenging the status quo almost immediately.

Salvation is Free

In this temple purging, Genesis moment He affirms, "Salvation is free!"

"So if the Son sets you free, you will be free indeed" (John 8:36)

Creation on a collision course,
Religious leaders decrying its source

Chaos, exchangers coming hither,
Selling God to the highest bidder.

Midst this infamous, historical heist,
Introducing Genesis, Jesus Christ!
Status quo, designed to impede,
Genesis thinkers: "FREE INDEED!"

The Salvation Army
...in its epochal Genesis years, dared courageously and with great conviction to sing and dance in the chaos beyond the culture that spawned its early pioneers.

In those years Great Britain was undergoing profound industrial change, chaotic in every respect. Mark Twain, while visiting London in 1897 for an event honoring the Queen, observed: "British history is two thousand years old and yet in a good many ways the world has moved farther ahead since the Queen was born than it moved in all the rest of the two thousand put together."

The Industrial Revolution

Twain's observation captures the sense of dizzying change characterizing this Victorian period, including a mass migration of workers to industrial towns, where ever-growing urban slums awaited them. Someone wrote, "The rhythm of the seasons was replaced by the rhythm of the water wheel and the steam engine." Women, youth and children comprised almost two-thirds of the manufacturing workforce.

Traditional ideas were being challenged, including the role of women in that society. Advances in the printing press during this period made information and knowledge more accessible to the masses, resulting in a more informed reading public, leading to controversy and debate on political and social issues.

And what about organized religion during this time? Findley Dunachie notes in his historical writings, "The church quiescent supports the status quo. In neither country was the established Church a force for change..."

Quiescent: Inactive or at rest. Dormant. Inert. (Encarta)

Passion: Fervor. Zeal. Enthusiasm. Commitment.

William Booth's passion for these displaced souls disturbed the quiescence of New Connexion Methodism greatly, so much so, that at their 1861 annual conference in Liverpool a decision was made to minimize the magnitude of his ministry. This action disquieted the soul of his wife, Catherine, so much so, that from the gallery, she spontaneously stood forth and cried out...

Never!

When Catherine said, "Never!" she was saying "Yes!" to Genesis and "No!" to status quo. This is one of those rare instances where the word, "No!" is appropriate because, in this case, a "yes" would have been a "no" to Genesis. In the same breath she said "No!" to culture and "Yes!" to need. Once again creation and culture collide!

Souls crying out in dizzying confusion
Two of them spiritually aware

Products of unwieldy, chaotic diffusion
Yielded together in prayer

Desperately seeking a healing infusion
Asking, "Who's out there to care?"
Viewed by some an unwanted intrusion.
Thus igniting her passion with flare!

NEVER!

This one word, felt passionately and delivered spontaneously, ignited a Genesis movement, unstoppable. Chaos is the incubator for creativity and innovation; Passion is its fuel and energy.

Passion: Spontaneous spiritual combustion (Noland).
Fast forward to the nearly present
Enter two leaders effervescent

Paul and Kay, worldwide bound
Finding the Army then quiescent
Yet the Spirit omnipresent
Fearlessly running, they hit the ground
Genesis, modus operandi
Passion, genius: "Do or die!"

Creativity, round and round
"Go for it!" the battle cry
Statistically, a spiritual high

For multitudes, a new life found

"GO FOR IT!"
Rader speak for...
"LET THERE BE!"

Lift Up Thine Eyes

"We Have Caught The Vision Splendid"

Richard Munn

The rest of the world saw a Florida marsh, fetid, good-for-nothing swampland. Walt Disney saw a Magic Kingdom with roller coasters, water parks and even a Cinderella Castle, where families would flock and have the holiday of a lifetime. Here was someone with a vision, a creative dream, and the rest, as they say, is history. Disney World in Florida is the most visited attraction in the world with attendance of over 50 million people annually.

Dreamers and Visionaries

In the 1,500 years it took to write the Bible, and in the 1,500 years following, believers considered visions a natural way in which the spiritual world broke into human life. God's revelation of Himself through visions and dreams is embraced by the early church fathers and such a concept is normative in their writings. It is only since the sophistication of the industrial age that people have become more skeptical. We can confidently say that through the years, dreams and visions are one of the most common ways that God communicates with human beings; and that to neglect or reject the visionaries can separate us from one of the most significant ways God wants to reach out to people. One of the painful disclosures in the book of Lamentations is that there are no more prophets — literally, no more "visionaries."

Richard Munn soldiers at the Glebe Corps in inner city Sydney. He first met the Raders as a cadet in the USA East, 1985-87, where they served as SFOT Principals. Their biggest influence was their inherent internationalism, egalitarian commitment and effective preaching ministry. Munn serves as Chief Secretary for Australia Eastern Territory, at the administrative crossroads of a vibrant and creative territory.

Could it be that visionary imagination is a gift from God; a gift that takes us beyond human experience and gives meaning and purpose, a gift of graphic communication from God himself? Through a vision we are reminded that there is something more than the material world and human reason.

It was President Kennedy who stimulated the scientific community and set an indelible vision for a man on the moon in 1961, saying, "We choose to go to the moon. We choose to go to the moon in this decade." And, it was Martin Luther King, Jr., who galvanized a people towards racial reconciliation with his 1963 "I have a dream" speech, with the evocative image "that my four little children will one day live in a nation where they will not be judged by the color of their skin, but by the content of their character." Decades later people are still inspired by the inherent power of those visions.

Vision In An Organization: The Symbolic Frame

In 1984 Bolman and Deal penned a bestseller, "Reframing Organizations," in which they categorized helpful ways to reassess corporate structures. One lens is the "Symbolic Frame," whereby organizations are depicted as tribes and in theatre and where the corporate values, product and culture are strategically propelled by pageantry, stories, heroes, and vision.

The Salvation Army is tailor made for the symbolic frame. The richness of her dramatic history is replete with legends and heroes. The symbolism of military motif and the thrill of spiritual warfare are abounding in dramatic imagery. The annual commissioning ceremonies and periodic congresses are irreplaceable in communicating the "big idea." They inspire people from local settings who may only infrequently see pageantry, and who are only familiar with their neighborhood scene. They connect people at an important and emotive level.

In the beginning it was the imagery and drama of belonging to an army that helped inspire the undisciplined and alienated to find purpose and mission in London's notorious east end; the same could be said of the shunned "criminal caste" people of India and the alcohol addled inhabitants of the Bowery in New York City.

In more contemporary organizational parlance, one that expresses the corporate essence of The Salvation Army, Commissioner Robert Watson would say such people are now "engaged in spirit."

The Visionary Leader

The visionaries who are able to communicate evocatively can prove transformative for the direction of a movement. They call us upward and onward, spurring us to imagine beyond current confines, and tapping into our innate human capacity for significance. Untapped reservoirs of creativity, energy and sacrifice now find a cause and a channel for outlet.

This cannot be forced or manufactured; people intuitively discern artifice; we instinctively recoil from concocted hyperbole. And so the vision and the visionary must also be grounded in the reality of the day, the experience of the people and the condition of the culture. And, they can see beyond. Kennedy and King got that absolutely right.

This necessarily creates what Dr. Wayne Goodwin, Gordon Conwell Theological Seminary, describes as the "burden of contradictory expectations." The leader is expected to oversee the global picture, but is evaluated negatively if he or she does not attend to details.

Biblical Visionaries

It will come as no surprise to find the Scriptures of the Old and New Testaments replete with visionaries. From the Hebrew Scriptures surely none can match Moses for sheer tenacity and accomplishment. With a people group subsumed by centuries of Egyptian slavery, it was only a divine vision that could lead him to say to Pharaoh "Let my people go," and to then repeatedly call forth the dream of "a land flowing with milk and honey." It took a generation to be accomplished.

The Davidic vision was for a temple in Jerusalem, captured by the picturesque insight that "I am living in a palace made of cedar wood, but the Ark of God is in a tent!" A generation later the dream was fulfilled.

The apostle John, exiled and isolated on the tiny Mediterranean island of Patmos, has a global vision in which "there before me was a great multitude that no one could count, from every nation, tribe, people and language, standing before the throne and in front of the Lamb." The paradox is sublime — punitive solitary confinement birthing the context for a polyglot multi-cultural vision, one still reverberating around the world, multiple generations later.

Of course, Jesus himself is the transcendent visionary, whether it is in the unscripted moments — calling Peter and Andrew to leave their nets behind and become "fishers of men" — or the grand, paradigm-shaking vision that "The time has come. The kingdom of God is near." Two thousand years later, both the personal and global vibrations of such calling forth are still unsettling swaths of people.

Wesleyan Optimism

"Wesleyan optimism" fundamentally nurtures a worldview of grace, one that is inherently cosmic. It knows no bounds. Its impact is impressive. The founder of Methodism, John Wesley, imbued with Biblical visionary scope, calmly asserted "The world is my parish," and then proceeded to spend more than 50 years in field and open air preaching, travelling 250,000 miles on horseback in the process, helping the vision come to fruition.

William Booth, gripped with a similar worldview, drafted his "Darkest England and the Way Out" scheme, beginning in the slums and gin houses of Victorian England, and culminating in "the colony across the sea" beckoning The Salvation Army on the horizon. At the time of his passing in 1912, The Salvation Army served in 46 countries around the world, with 235,000 soldiers.

More recently, on the eve of a new millennium, General Paul and Commissioner Kay Rader were able to articulate in evocative and picturesque language, the global vision of a "million marching" for the worldwide Salvation Army. At the time the international number of soldiers was 835,000; how significant to hear the public announcement during the 2000 Millennial Congress in Atlanta, Georgia, that the army now had 1.01 million soldiers.

Parenthetically, the Raders stimulated a call to global prayer with the image of "an army on its knees." The phrase captured the imagination of Salvationists and channelled through the epochal "International Spiritual Life Commission," whose work is still influencing The Salvation Army, over a decade later.

The sheer dreams of all four are out of this world, almost literally.

Lift Up Thine Eyes

"Vision is the art of seeing what is invisible to others," wrote Jonathan Swift. In the grit and grind of much human endeavor, it is a vision beyond the immediate that can enliven and galvanize us.

The popular American artist Norman Rockwell captures this elusiveness in his portrayal of a bustling New York City street scene in which a solitary and dutiful clergyman is piecing together his Sunday sermon title on the outdoor bulletin board, "Lift Up Thine Eyes." Every passer-by is looking downward, pressing on with the duty of the day.

The visionary looks up, and calls us to a more grand and glorious reality.

Yes indeed, we lift up our eyes.

The Imperative of Mission

"Onward Christian Soldiers"

Ronald G. Irwin

I t could be argued that the most important impact made by Paul Rader, both as territorial commander in the USA West and as the international leader of The Salvation Army, was his insistence that the Army be mission-focused and that this focus dominate its ministry and activities. During his term of office in the Western Territory, it resulted in an evangelistic thrust called MISSION2000, which called all Salvationists to seek the unchurched (particularly "baby boomers"), to open new corps, and to develop new nontraditional expressions of Salvation Army corps ministry in order to reach new generations for Christ. In addition, Rader insisted the territory use its resources of money and personnel more effectively to enhance mission.

As the General, Paul Rader issued a call for 1,000,000 senior soldiers in the International Salvation Army—a goal reached in 1999, the year of his retirement! He understood that a zealous, intense emphasis on mission would produce measurable mission results, and would fulfill the Great Commission given by Christ to His disciples to " … go and make disciples … and teach them to obey …" (Matt. 28:19-20).

When I was a young officer, there was not much talk about mission in the Army. There was no carefully crafted "mission statement." Instead there was a mind-set that suggested officers needed to "maintain" the work to which they had been assigned, obey regulations, stay out of debt, and keep certain standards of meetings and activities.

Ronald Irwin soldiers at the Clearwater, Florida Corps, where he serves as songster pianist. Irwin's relationship with Paul Rader goes back to the early 1950's where he worked with him on summer camp staff. Later he was Rader's field training officer at the Astoria Corps. Finally, Irwin served as Rader's Chief Secretary in USA West, before returning to USA East as its territorial leader. It was here where significant growth occurred through the "People-Our Priority" mission initiative.

But with the focus on mission, led by Paul Rader and a few like-minded stalwarts, the Army was forced to consider its mission roots and the need to apply resources so they would produce mission results.

The early name of The Army, The Christian Mission, reflected our fundamental nature and purpose. "Mission" described why we were raised up as an evangelistic force, and certainly accounts for the swift progress of the Army in establishing itself as an international Army. Albert Orsborn was right when he said the Army is a "permanent mission to the unconverted." William Booth was right when he said, "The Christian Mission is a Salvation Army." But the reverse is also true: "The Salvation Army is a Christian Mission!"

That is why every territorial commander, every divisional commander, every officer, whether on the front lines or in the various headquarters, must make certain all effort is expended to keep a clear mission-focus, to make certain the Army is not drifting, doing things that are unproductive that do not contribute to mission objectives, because every officer in every appointment is given a sacred trust and is accountable to God and the Army to produce mission results.

The mission is not the officer's mission—it is God's mission realized through the officer in the Army, dependent on officers clearly understanding they must be in alignment with the mission outlined so succinctly by General Gowans in the February 2001 issue of *The Officer* magazine:

to save souls
to produce saints
to serve suffering humanity.

Now in order to carry out mission, officers must understand nothing is fixed permanently. This means every generation of Army leaders must deal with the present and cannot be tied down by past decisions, which once served a useful purpose but are no longer relevant. This is because structure must serve mission. Where structure inhibits changes to better serve mission, it is defective, not sacred, and causes obsolescence, irrelevance and lack of mission progress.

It is not throwing out structure — structure is essential in preventing chaos and keeping things orderly and tidy, helping to define the Army as a movement. But often mission effectiveness requires new methodology to meet ever-changing, new situations, demanding a structure that promotes mission objectives. Structure must be adjusted to serve mission while still maintaining Army principles and cohesiveness.

William Booth talked about "continuity of principle, with constant adaptation to change," describing the Army's mission by saying "… it is not the doing of certain duties, the maintenance of particular beliefs, or the conducting of special meetings, important as those may be, but…an intelligent, practical partnership with God in the business of saving the world."

To accomplish this, Booth said:

We have been trying to break loose all the trammels of custom and propriety which may in any degree have hindered or hampered in the past ... We mean to gain the ear of the people for our Master, and we are more than ever determined that no conformity to any church forms or ideas shall hinder us.

He said:

Beginning as I did with a clean sheet of paper, wedded to no plan ... willing to take a leaf out of anybody's book…above all, to obey the direction of God the Holy Spirit ... we tried various methods and those that did not answer we unhesitatingly threw overboard and adopted something else.

Bramwell Booth is quoted as saying:

No organization may remain rigid and inflexible. It must be modified by natural evolution, adapting itself continually to new conditions. Though the spirit does not change, the form and method by which it is clothed must change.

From the very beginning of the Army, mission was linked to

methodology. Questions asked were: How do we best accomplish mission? What needs to be done to achieve mission objectives? What must be done to get mission results?

To William Booth, whatever did not produce mission results was discarded! Something else was tried. Flexibility and adaptability were essential. Constant evaluation of results was standard practice. Booth wanted to know how effectively his methods worked. Mission was paramount! It is what must be paramount in the Army today!

It must be understood that a Salvation Army officer/leader cannot be mission minded if…

Rules are more important than what they produce
Control is more important than trust and empowerment
Processes more important than results
Compliance more important than flexibility
Form more important than substance
Commanding more important than leading
Regulation more important than mission
Doing things right more important than doing the right thing
Personal agenda more important than the larger picture
Recognition more important than productivity
Methodology more important than mission
Rank/title/position more important than competence and servanthood… because structure always must serve mission!

Methodology must further mission objectives. Systems must facilitate achieving mission goals. Controls must protect mission objectives. The officer leader must not mix efforts with results—working hard at the wrong thing is no virtue. Officers must be accountable for mission results, not efforts! Resources must be invested in mission, not in personal entitlements or in "machinery!"

Producing a vision statement or inaugurating a program such as MISSION2000 or the Eastern Territory's PEOPLE – OUR PRIORITY initiative, or any other effort designed to stimulate mission is only the first step. Articulation of a mission plan is not enough.

There also must be a plan of action, and there must be a constant, regular revisiting of the plan. There must be measurable goals for which officers (and particularly the leaders of officers) must be held accountable. Vision and mission initiatives, once articulated, must not be allowed to be filed away, neglected, considered distractions, or ignored. Accountability for mission results should be demanded — and this requires persistence and the constant reminder of mission imperatives because any leader who articulates a mission plan without vigorously promoting the plan or insisting on accountability loses respect and is not taken seriously.

… If the mission of the Army, in partnership with Christ, is to preach the Gospel of Jesus Christ and to meet human needs in His name without discrimination

… and if the mission of the Army, in partnership with Christ, is to fulfill the Great Commission to get people saved, keep people saved so they can get other people saved, and to train them to be disciples who can be sent to carry out the mission … then every Officer/Leader must be prepared to answer these critical questions:

What is my mission battle plan?
How does it shape my work?
How much of my time is invested in the plan?
How does it affect my decisions?
How do I evaluate effectiveness?
Is it producing measurable mission results?

Every officer, no matter the appointment, must resolve to be mission-productive, not maintenance-minded, so that when officers farewell, they are able to answer "yes" to these critical questions:

• Did I cause this appointment to grow in mission specifics?
• Did I develop the people I supervised and led?
• Did I find new, better ways to accomplish old, familiar tasks?
• Did I raise the level of quality?
• Did I improve structure efficiency?

- Did I invest resources in mission?
- DID I GET THE JOB DONE?

These are questions every officer, no matter the appointment, must ask because every officer must get the job done and be mission productive, driven by a burning conviction that as an officer, covenanted and ordained, commissioned to preach the Gospel and win souls, the officer is accountable to God and the Army for measurable Mission results!

Paul Rader was right on target when he insisted that the Army be mission focused!

John Gowans, his successor as General, whole-heartedly embraced the focus. His impassioned words in *The Officer* (Feb. 2001) shall serve as the exclamation point to this chapter:

"I feel we are being led by the Spirit to major in missions! To do this we need to coldly, even ruthlessly – but certainly prayerfully – examine the way in which we invest our human and monetary resources, our energy and our gifts as a movement in the light of the question "Does what we are doing really further our mission?"

"And then we must find the courage to jettison the useless in preference for the useful!" This must be a continuing examination.

> The question needs to be constantly faced: Is this the best way to achieve one or the other of these paramount ambitions (to save souls, to produce saints, to serve suffering humanity)? If the answer is no or not really, then we must find the courage to change what needs to be changed.

The Salvation Army must major in missions!

Boundless

"O Boundless Salvation"

Danielle Strickland

While we are motivated by great optimism as to the possibility for change and new life for persons and communities, we are not naive regarding the fallenness and sinfulness of the human heart. Nor are we unaware of the evil desire of Satan to deceive and destroy, to demean and damn human persons. Further, we accept that there can be a powerful and pervasive demonic dimension evident in human systems and structures, institutions and cultures. We are called to live out our faith and pursue our mission in a fallen world that may put us at risk. All the more we are determined not to back down from any overt or insidious challenge to Christ's kingdom, whether that challenge is in the form of personalized or institutionalized evil.—General Paul A. Rader

My early understanding of The Salvation Army was pretty small; it was limited by what I knew and whom I knew in my own sphere of influence. Before the advent of the Internet that allows us to peek into the daily happenings of the global world...we lived sheltered and small lives of Salvationism.

The thing is, the same problem I had in my limited vision within The Salvation Army is the disease I caught from a Christian culture that had done the same thing to the Gospel. The Raders were people with eyes wide open to the possibilities of the "world for God" and the realities of the fight needed in this present age.

Danielle Strickland soldiers at Crossroads Corps in Edmonton, Canada. She has been inspired by the Raders' tenacious, shared leadership, their passionate preaching, missionary sacrifice, and stubborn persistence toward their convictions. She first encountered Commissioner Kay Rader at a women's holiness conference. Strickland's role in the salvation war these days involves evangelizing, discipling, teaching, and pioneering work among marginalized women.

They embodied a life that actually lived out this reality in their officership, in their callings, partnerships, and their commitments—all leveraged to seeing that happen. Rather than a small focus or hoping just to maintain the existing structures and establishment, the Raders helped unleash the possibilities and bolster the Army's fight against sin and for justice.

Actually, I think it might have been an "old" way of thinking, all the way back to the way The Salvation Army started: as a visionary movement of covenanted warriors ready and willing to win the whole world for Jesus. This aggressive movement always needs leadership that sees the aim as mobilization and forward advance. I know I do.

You can buy a Bible in a North American Christian book shop that substitutes your name where all the promises of God are... for example John 3:16 will read "for God so loved (fill your name in here) that he gave us His Son." At first glance this is kind of heart warming and nice. I mean, it fits with a popular worship song that suggests that what Jesus was thinking about on the cross was of course, "me" (above all). Wow! Although, at first glance, this is true — God does love me and salvation is deeply personal — there is something missing to the message. This is a small Gospel.

Recently, I was trying to get my two-year-old son to take some medicine. He wasn't interested. I tried a variety of techniques of persuasion (bribing, scolding, pleading among them) but finally resorted to the old "force it down" option. I held him down with my knee across his chest and my eldest son held his head and we grabbed the syringe filled with banana flavored penicillin and shoved it down his throat. We did it because we loved him and wanted him to be healthy. While that episode was unfolding I sensed the Spirit of the living God speak to me about how I present the Gospel, how I even understand the Gospel. Too often I struggled to squeeze enough Gospel into people to get them to heaven, without realizing the power of the Gospel to break into dark and desperate places in order that the light might shine brightly throughout the entire earth.

See, I have a hunch that my Gospel smallness is a problem with many more people than me. And this problem has resulted in sharing a small god with a very limited impact. As a result of this tiny Gospel, salvation with a very small "s"—we have limited salvation to be about my life, my family my neighborhood. God reminded me of the bigness of the plan of salvation. God's plan of salvation is not just to inoculate some folks who are in need of saving...it's not a survival strategy or a system by which we can be well for ourselves.

God's plan, as it has always been, is to redeem the whole earth. To fix the brokenness at the heart of the world, to reverse the effects of sin, to break the curse and the powers of darkness. His plan is a liberating of the entire created order. Think of it and remind yourself that John 3:16 does not even suggest that it's simply the world that God loved but the Greek word used in the verse is the entire "cosmos." God so loved the entire created order. Think of it just a second.

And then think on the ramifications. If God's plan of salvation is larger than my little life then how does my life matter? And this is where the smallness connects to the vastness of this salvation plan. My life matters because God's plan to redeem the earth includes me. This is the radical notion of Jesus' invitation to all disciples. His invitation is not simply to have Him join us to make our lives better. Actually, He suggests in the Gospel accounts that the reverse of that is true. We will be "saved" but our lives might become more difficult, even unto death. But His declaration, His incarnation, His death and resurrection was and is to change the world. To disturb the present in order to bring a new future, as Catherine Booth suggested.

And His outlandish invitation is to use us to do it. To use the smallness of our ordinary, everyday lives to actually storm the forts of darkness and bring them down. That is the power of the early disciples—they finally realized that the plan was bigger than them. Freedom is just another word for nothing left to lose (Janet Joplin sang that but I think she got it from the Gospels). The same is true for the early Salvationists and many others just like them as they enter into the largeness of God's plan for boundless salvation to the ends of the earth.

They are saved, surely from themselves but not for themselves.

They are saved for the salvation of the world. They are an Army on the march and they will not back down! We can grow stronger everyday if we believe the Raders' life example and give ourselves, all of ourselves, over to this oceanic calling, this boundless salvation. I pray that we will catch this revelation, or rather the revelation will catch us, much like the Apostle John on the Island of Patmos, realizing afresh what the huge presence of Jesus means to the ends of the world. I pray that out of God's unlimited resources He may strengthen you with power in your inner being so that you can grasp just how wide, and long and high and deep is the love of God (Ephesians 3 prayer).

What is fun about this reminder is that Catherine and William Booth had already caught this idea and embodied it in The Salvation Army. Far from a conventional church that was trying to grow congregations that cared for themselves, the Booths started a movement of people that were aggressively taking new ground for God. They heard and were responding to the cries of oppressed people around the earth who were crying out for liberation and freedom. Salvation inside and out. And William Booth recognized that this was the large plan of God; he penned it in the words of a song he called *Boundless Salvation*. One of the phrases really hit me that day: "the whole world redeeming."

The Son came to destroy the devil's work (1 John 3:8). That's a job description if ever I heard it. It's the job description for Jesus. He didn't come just to think of me and love me and make my life better, although all that happens when Jesus shows up. He came to redeem the earth. To make a sacrifice that once and for all would break a curse that was destroying the earth. He came to set the captives free and that means in today's world at least 27 million people enslaved in the largest slave trade known in history—human trafficking.

In General Rader's comment you can hear the echo of early Salvationists with this aggressive understanding of salvation but also a large context for a large God who can do anything and everything through wholly submitted people—risking their lives and their limbs and their reputations and their future for the lost and the broken and the oppressed. I suppose this spirit that runs rampant in the writings and the actions of the primitive Salvationists is the same spirit that ran loose in and through Jesus. It's the Holy Spirit who is reminding us and rebuking us every time we make the Gospel simply a personal choice and a personal salvation, as though Jesus is merely our personal savior. He is the savior of the whole earth. He is the savior of the lost. He means to redeem the inside and the outside of the entire created order.

So this big plan, this salvation plan is the one I mean to give my life to. I think the example of the Raders is helpful on this point, not just what they said but how they lived. Consistently challenging small systems and thinking, choosing to live another way to give their lives for the Gospel that is for the entire world. Even their commitment to really live an egalitarian partnership, a marriage devoted to a larger plan. Together they became more instead of two becoming less. This is evidence of their deep understanding of salvation being larger than their own lives. To live in other cultures, to see the bigness of the world, to challenge existing structures and systems that would try to limit and control the Spirit of God at work in The Salvation Army.

May God give us the boundless vision necessary to live large lives in order that The Salvation Army might bring redemption to the earth.

The Great Commission

"The World For God"

Peter H. Chang

As Christians, we are mindful of the command our good Lord has given us, his final commission to all His followers to preach the Gospel to win souls for His Kingdom. This is clearly recorded in each of the four Gospels: Matthew 28: 16-20; Mark 16:14-16; Luke 24: 44-49; John 20: 19-23.

While this is very clear, we often encounter some good Christians remarking: "When there is so much work to be done in our own land, how can we possibly go further out into the world?" Did Jesus not say we should be witnesses in Jerusalem, in all Judea and Samaria and to the ends of the earth? It is a very valid point these folks are making but not what our Lord was saying. He did not command, "When you evangelize Jerusalem completely, then go to all Judea and to Samaria, then to the ends of the world." No: He was meaning for us to spread out from where we are in our own country, to neighboring places, then elsewhere to the ends of the world. After all, if we waited until the whole of Jerusalem is completely won for the Lord, there would not be any witnesses in any other part of the world at all.

How very grateful I am that those early-day followers went out immediately to the ends of the earth so that, in time, the Gospel reached Korean shores. Especially, I naturally would like to mention corps growth in The Salvation Army, not only in the Korea Territory but also in the USA Western Territory where it also was my privilege to serve.

Peter Chang, who soldiers at San Diego ARC, invests himself in intercessory prayer and leading young students. He followed Rader as territorial leader of the USA Western Territory, and has known them both since their first appointment in Korea. They worked together on Training College Staff. Chang reflects, "Their friendship, strong conviction, and determination of Mission has been a resounding influence."

According to historians, the Gospel reached Korea via China through Roman Catholics, around 1784, which was almost 100 years before the first Protestant missionary, Reverend Horace Allen, reached Korea in 1884. By the time The Salvation Army arrived in 1908, other Christian churches were more or less well established. Though there had been an outpouring of the Holy Spirit that saw the Gospel message spread and God's church growing, there had not been any such organized church growth as experienced in modern expressions elsewhere around the world.

During the late 1960s, church growth efforts had ignited, much through the efforts of the Fuller Theological Seminary in California, USA. It caught fire in Korea in the mid 1970s.

The Salvation Army Korea Territory has had many dedicated and outstanding missionaries: altogether there have been 157 such people, coming from such places as the United Kingdom, Scandinavia, the USA, Australia and New Zealand as well. There are many wonderfully-inspiring stories of missionaries in Korea but, among them all, particularly when church growth is mentioned, the names of Paul and Kay Rader should also be recorded: the same Paul Rader who was later elected the General of The Salvation Army. Early in 1970, Paul Rader attended the Fuller Theological Seminary, studying and earning his degree as a Doctor of Missiology.

Let me first mention the family background. Of course, Paul is deeply rooted as a Salvationist, with officers on both his mother's and his father's sides. His parents, Lieutenant-Colonel & Mrs. Lyell Rader OF, brought up their five children in the faith, all becoming missionaries in various parts of the world. It is like a living family commission: with Jeanne and her husband, Doctor Ted Gabrielson, serving in Korea; Damon in Zimbabwe and Zambia, Africa; Paul in Korea; Herbert in Zimbabwe, Africa; and Lyell in Sri Lanka. During one special occasion when all the family members came together to celebrate, someone commented to Mrs. Lieutenant-Colonel Gladys Rader how difficult it must be to have all the children away from home. She simply, yet sincerely, responded: "I would rather have them far away from me yet in the center of His will; than have them all near and around me, out of His will." What a marvelous testimony and living great commission the Rader family is!

As mentioned, in the middle of the 1970s church growth caught fire in Korea and, of course, The Salvation Army also seized the moment. How fortunate it was that Paul was there to assist with the corps growth of the territory. He did it well too, not appearing at the helm of the venture but by staying in the background, steering and providing excellent support and assistance with the success of this program to the then Territorial Commander, Commissioner Chun, Yong-sup.

In order to provide the necessary funding for the new corps that were opening, the territory established a revolving fund to loan money to the various corps for new openings. Initially, there was no such money on hand, so the assistance of international headquarters was sought. The then chief of the staff, Commissioner Arthur E. Carr, was so impressed with the concept that he approved the revolving fund money as a grant. However, the then International Secretary, Commissioner W. Stanley Cottrill, preferred to honor the loan as requested, so it became a loan. Having this funding available made it much easier for the territory in its operation of new corps commencing. In time, the loan was fully and completely paid back to international headquarters through the assistance of the USA Western Territory, with then Commissioner Paul A. Rader as the territorial commander.

As of 2013, 11% of active officers of the Korea Territory are serving in 14 different countries overseas. That is 71 of the 622 officers and includes those officers who have immigrated to the land where they serve.

The amazing thing is that, despite inevitable leadership changes in the territory, the strategic plan has still carried on. Now, under the banner of The Salvation Army Territorial Vision 2028 Hope Project, further goals have been set for the year 2028. This is phenomenal. Certainly we keenly observe how the territory continues to progress and how the Hope Project is fulfilled by the designated year 2028.

Meanwhile, in the Christian Church in the Republic of Korea, more than 12,000 missionaries have been sent to 160 countries;

compared with 46,000 American and 6,000 British missionaries, according to statistics available to missionary organizations in South Korea and around the western world.

The following gives a comparison of statistical detail related to corps growth in the Korea Territory between 1974 and 1991:

As of 31st December	1974	1991
Number of Corps	93	191
Number of Senior Soldiers	15,783	31,599
Number of Junior Soldiers	6,084	8,027
Officers (active)	209	447
Officers (retired)	33	57
Sunday meeting attendances	14,973	27,847

Now let's turn our focus to the USA Western Territory.

When Commissioner Paul Rader completed his first year as leader of the Territory, he made the decision to establish the goal of MISSION2000 (see the *New Frontier,* March 14, 1991).

In setting this goal, the figure was not pulled out of the air. Commissioner Paul Rader used a consultative approach with middle-level leaders, (namely the divisional commanders through the assistant chief secretary), asking how many new corps they envisioned opening in the division over the next 10 years. He asked how that goal could be reached or why more could not be reached and, pressing further, how it could be achieved in each division. If the leader himself was the problem, then the leader was changed. Should the leader have needed more financial help or any other assistance, then he was supported and helped. In the Hawaiian Islands, for instance, there were no more possibilities for growth, yet the divisional commander responded that 10 new corps would be opened during the next decade. The obvious questions were raised: "Where?" and "How?" The response was to open new corps on neighboring islands, e.g., the Marshall Islands and Guam, with the necessary financial assistance. Having caught the leader's vision, Commissioner Rader readily approved and supported the plan.

A total of 115 new corps were scheduled to open in the existing divisions at that time. Corps Growth and Evangelism Secretary, Captain Terry Camsey, who had also just completed his church growth course at Fuller Seminary, was given responsibility for opening an additional 35 new corps.

Once the goal of MISSION2000 was established, the plan was checked and monitored annually by territorial leaders who continued to receive progress reports from the divisional commanders.

The Victory Congress of 1997 was planned to celebrate a special three-year-long campaign of PEOPLE COUNT, which aimed to increase the size of the corps, along with MISSION2000. When the goal of MISSION 2000 was reached early, the USA Western Territory celebrated the Victory Congress, coordinated by then Captains (and now Commissioners) Kenneth G. and Jolene Hodder, in June 1997, and led by General Paul A. Rader and Commissioner Kay Rader.

Lieutenant-Colonel Doug O'Brien provided the 1997 statistics, as totaled and finalized in 1998, comparing the facts with ten years prior.

- The number of corps rose from 204 to 307, an increase of 103

- Senior soldiership rose from 13,773 to 17,718, an increase of 3,945

In the June 30, 1997 *New Frontier,* Robert Docter reported an attendance of 8,250 at the Victory Congress, with 1,600 new senior and junior soldiers sworn-in by the General.

It truly was a most exciting congress: the spirit was victorious, the morale of the territory was victorious and, most of all, the message was victorious. To Him be the victory! To Him be the glory!

Such growth can only be sustained through effective leadership at the corps level, as well as at the divisional and territorial level. Only then will the territory continue to grow, under the blessing of the Lord, as we continue our efforts on behalf of The Great Commission.

A Million Marching
"On We March"

Royston Bartlett

A million marching into the new millennium: wholly committed to Christ and to the colors!

Nobody would be in conversation with General Paul Rader (R) for very long before they were made aware that he believes that The Salvation Army is a powerful instrument in the hand of God for world evangelization. Writing in *The Officer* Magazine in September 1995 he said:

> Our world is crying out in pain. Heroic Salvationists who have gone before us have garnered the confidence of people by dint of their sacrificial devotion to the neediest of the earth. We are, perhaps, the world's most widely dispersed, deeply experienced and effectively organized Christian-humanitarian agency. Our hurting world needs the Army—in strength!

This then was the motivating drive of the Raders for the Army to have a million soldiers marching into the new millennium. However, there were several other factors that led to General Rader projecting that goal for the Army toward the year 2000. Senior Soldiery was just at 800,000 when he took office.

It seemed to the General that looking toward the year 2000, a goal of 1,000,000, particularly given the rapid growth of the Army in Africa and Asia, was challenging but attainable and might capture the imagination of Salvationists.

Royston Bartlett, who soldiers at the Bromley Temple Corps, United Kingdom Territory, met the Raders when the General appointed him as his ADC. Bartlett states, "It is said that a General is not a hero to his ADC. Not true. General Paul Rader is my hero!" As a retired officer he is involved, part time, in the officer appointment system for the UKI Territory. Bartlett's claim to fame: "That I met Princess Diana and had a ten minute conversation with her! We simply liked each other!" He has also sung with all the major choirs in London and one in Stockholm.

The General had been long committed to growth, as his term in USA Western Territory would testify to any student's scrutiny. Substantive and sustainable growth depended on an increase of senior soldiers. Adherency seemed to be growing in acceptance, and it was and is an important option. But adherents do not constitute "fighting units," with few exceptions. It takes soldiers to make an Army.

Further, General Rader believed then that adherency left those concerned short of a public confession of their faith in Christ and the functional equivalent of baptism. So there were strategic and theological incentives toward establishing a challenging goal for strengthening the soldier ranks.

Within a year of the Raders taking their international leadership roles the *Spiritual Life Commission* had been summoned to attend to the inner life of the Army. The Raders wanted soldiers fully alive in Christ, actively committed to the Army's mission, and as the General indicated in the Vision Statement that came a few years later he wanted an Army fully alive in Christ, pure in heart, united in purpose, aflame with a passion for God and souls.

General Rader has said:

In many Western countries there is a powerful cultural resistance to organizational commitment. Volunteers are available, but on their own terms, and only for limited engagements. Serious, unconditional commitment for the long haul is simply out of the question in many quarters. They just don't want to belong. Attending is one thing, accepting the disciplines of soldiership, quite another. Adherency is good, it brings people under the sound of the Gospel and places them well within reach of the pastoral care of the corps. But in and of itself, it is not the stuff of an Army. Congregations are one thing, commitment, another.

During the many visits to the Army world by General Paul Rader and Commissioner Kay Rader they were able first hand to meet thousands of dedicated and loyal marching Salvationists. Observing these marching Salvationists — was this yet another inspiration to for the Raders to see the million marching towards 2000?

To stand on a podium in Kenya and watch the thousands upon thousands of Salvationists marching past to salute their General was such a huge privilege. As the ADC to the General it was not uncommon for me to stand behind the General supporting his arm as he saluted the marching Salvationists. The march seemed endless.

On a visit to the Democratic Republic of Congo Territory to hear the band playing *All Have Need of God's Salvation* as the countless Salvationists marched past the international leaders, each marching Salvationist clutching tightly a Bible in the one hand and saluting the General with the other. Tears flowed from our eyes as they marched and sang in French:

> *And this word it reaches Nations:*
> *Not the rich or learned or clever*
> *Only shall by him be rescued,*
> *O praise God! 'Tis whosoever.*

It was in that moment I whispered to the General, "We are here today to witness this only because we said 'Yes' to Christ when he called us into ministry." The General agreed!

A few days later the General's party went down to the River Congo to take the ferry across the water to the Congo (Brazzaville) Territory. As we left the quay thousands of loyal Salvationists had gathered to say farewell and the band played *We're a band that shall conquer the foe* to the shouts of Praise God and Hallelujah from the people. The ferry sailed out into the fast flowing tide and very soon we could hear the band on the other side playing the same message of the liberating love of God and the waiting Salvationists singing a welcome to their beloved international leaders.

During the visit a planned march was arranged but on the morning this was to take place a monsoon had arrived and the wind and rain fell in torrents. News kept on coming to the General that the march should be cancelled, but the Raders knew how enthusiastic the Salvationists were and how much they had looked forward to the march. However, the rain insisted on showing great power and in the end the march was cancelled. However, that didn't mean a thing. On this occasion the dedicated, loyal Salvationists had planned to march, they had looked forward to it and they were going to march, even if it meant disobeying the territorial leader's instruction!

As the General's party was preparing to leave the auditorium for the hotel drums could be faintly heard, getting louder and louder, then the various bands started to play and the General's party had to make a mad dash to the podium because the Salvationists were determined to march past their General, never mind the rain falling in torrents. So the General's party, even with coats and umbrellas, were soaked as the General took the salute to the marching Salvationists.

But not only in Africa but in Asia also and making their first visit to the India South Eastern Territory the Raders visited the Army's medical center at Nagercoil. At the hospital, eager Salvationists shouted "Hallelujah!" and waved banners, then a band appeared heading a march. To say the uniforms were of varied description would be an understatement, as would the instruments being played.

Jostled by the marching clamoring throng, as General Rader and Commissioner Kay Rader made their way from the front gate of the compound to the main hospital building, everyone reached out to touch them. One woman stepped forward and kissed their hands; others knelt to touch their shoes as they passed.

Seeing the mass of delighted people and witnessing their desire simply to touch our international leaders brought to my mind a picture of Jesus surrounded by a pressing throng. The old Gospel song resounded in my heart:

She only touched the hem of his garment
As to his side she stole, amid the crowds that
Gathered around him and straightway she was whole.

That moment in the life of Jesus, when the woman in the crowd reached out and touched the hem of the cloak of Jesus became real to me at the hospital in Nagercoil.

The General, in his message at Nagercoil, spoke of the day a man stretched out his hand to Jesus. At the conclusion, in the cool of the evening, the General encouraged his listeners to stretch out their hands in like manner to Christ.

Many came forward to kneel in prayer. Women, some in beautiful saris while others in well-worn saris, stretched out their hands to Jesus. Men knelt with heads bowed while cadets with open Bibles knelt alongside the seekers, encouraging them to search the truths found in the Gospel of Christ. In that moment I knew that God's plan for the salvation of the world had happened—the Gospel message, as told by the Army, had reached even to this area in southern India.

A million marching into the new millennium wholly committed to Christ and to the colors was the desire of General Paul Rader and Commissioner Kay Rader. The General knew that it was easy enough for him to project a numerical goal for growth. But what lies behind the desire for increased numbers? What is the motivation? He did wonder should the Army not rather downsize to Gideon-like devotion in our Army? Is not the quality of the force far more critical than the numerical strength of it? He agreed to all that, but he still felt led to call for a major commitment to the recruitment of senior soldiers around the world.

So the last words must go back to General Paul Rader (R):

A million marching cannot be achieved without a focused, prayer-powered, creatively strategized and energetically pursued effort in every territory and command of the world. Indeed, in every corps and center!

The Devil's Playground

"On We March"

Guy Noland

I recently had the privilege of interviewing General Paul and Commissioner Kay Rader for "Hard Corps," a feature-length documentary focused on exposing the truth behind mainstream pornography and how it relates to human sex trafficking (produced by SAVN.tv/ USA West). Even in retirement, General Paul sits on the board of Pure Hope, a ministry dedicated to providing Christian solutions to a sexualized world, and Commissioner Kay serves with RAAP (Religious Alliance Against Pornography) dedicating many precious hours to fighting the good fight.

The Raders have led the charge in the struggle against human sex trafficking, blazing a holy trail for Salvationists of all ages to follow. From where does this passion flow? Here are a few disturbing facts that may help to shed light on an answer:

- The national average for a young male's introduction to pornography is 9 years of age.

- 40% of parents surveyed report being greatly concerned about their teen's possible exposure to Internet porno graphy, exceeding concerns about potential depression, alcohol, cigarettes, drug abuse, and violence from the other teens.

Guy Noland soldiers at the Pasadena Tabernacle. He first met the Raders in the 1990's, as territorial leaders in USA West. He was privileged to be part of the team that produced their "Farewell Salute" from the West, sending them off to IHQ as international leaders. Noland reflects, "General Paul and Commissioner Kay have stood head and shoulders above most Salvation Army leaders during their career, stepping forth as mavericks in the truest sense. As true warriors for Christ, they never once shied away from the risk-taking necessary to advance the Gospel message. Their bravery stood as a shining example for us, the younger generation, to follow." Noland is the Executive Director/Producer of SAVN. tv (Salvation Army Vision Network) — www.savn.tv.

- A study of 30 adolescent sexual offenders (showed 29) were first exposed to pornography by age 7. Deviant sexual fantasies began at age 9 (on average). 87% committed sexual offenses at 10 years of age.

- A recent study reported 9 out of 10 young men and 1 out of 3 young women admit to using pornography.

- The average onset for pornography addiction occurs within 2.5 weeks of regular usage.

- The age at which the average male seeks help for pornography addiction is 35 years old.

- Do you find these statistics unsettling? I do. Just 20 years ago these types of statistics were unheard of. Where will we be 20 years from now?

In recollection of my youth, it occurred to me that we (Generation X) had minimal exposure to mainstream pornography. As children, pornography encompassed the dirty magazines propped behind the counter at the drug store, wrapped in plastic and out of arms reach. As for pornographic videos, my friends and I could not have ventured an educated guess as to where one would procure such media. Point of fact, in order to obtain adult entertainment, one had to risk public exposure by braving the "naughty room" in the back of a video store. We kids didn't dare step behind that curtain. Instead, we settled for the National Geographic centerfold and the women's underwear section of a Sears' catalogue.

These mild and not-so-pornographic anecdotes may seem comical, but the term "pornography addiction" didn't exist in our world. Nowadays it's an afterthought, a buzzword, a punch line.

Our generation was weaned on TV, a media controlled by the few and censored by the FCC. This generation (Millennial) was weaned on the Internet, a media controlled by the individual and censored by no one. It's a free-for-all of worldly expression, free speech, and sexual commendation with little parental control or fear of censure. If ever there existed the perfect soil for Satan to plant his seed and masterfully carry the world into hell, the Internet has won the blue ribbon. To be sure, it's the devil's playground.

The above opening statistics represent but a drop in the bucket of disturbing societal survey reports stemming from widespread Internet pornography abuse. Are you ready for the most mind-blowing statistic of all?

- 40% of religious leaders polled admitted to finding nothing wrong with the recreational use of pornography.

I know what you're thinking, "How is this possible? How can ANY ordained man or woman of God fail to see the lustful abuse of women perpetrated in pornography and deem it anything other than sinful?" The Enemy holds great sway over this world; so much so, even God's own people grow blind to blatant perversion.

So, what do we do about this scourge?

To (mis) quote William Booth, "Why should the devil have all the good [media]?" Simply put, we must stop viewing the Internet as a self-serving mode of entertainment and begin viewing it as the ultimate means of evangelism. We must rip away that which Satan holds dear and apply it to our own arsenal.

A missionary returning from a recent trip to Africa reported that even the most remote tribes in the country own cell phones. These people represent the poorest of the poor in our world. They have no electricity, no running water or plumbing, but they will walk two days to charge their cell phones on a car battery so as to maintain Internet access.

What does this mean? It means we have instant access to the ENTIRE world at the click of a mouse button! If we, as Christians and Salvationists, fail to use such a gift for evangelistic purposes, we fall short of fulfilling the Great Commission of Christ — go into ALL the world and spread the Gospel of Jesus Christ.

Yet another disturbing fact: Baby Boomers and Gen Xers currently carry the torch, providing critical financial support for our great Army. In 20-30 years, we will be dead and dying off, at which point it will fall to the Millennials to pick up the torch and carry on. If The Salvation Army has failed to meet them at their point of need (online) and failed to reach them with the Gospel where they live and congregate (online), they will have no course or desire to support our movement. Our Army will suffer depletion like never before.

When Willie Sutton, the prolific American bank robber, was asked why he robbed banks, he answered, "Because that's where the money is." The same can be said about our Founder, William Booth. In 19th century England there was no Internet, TV, X-box, or modern distractions. In as such, the average citizen took to the street corner as a meeting place to drink, socialize, and pass the time. General Booth recognized the need and created the "Church of the Open Air." He preached the Good News of Jesus Christ on the street corner because that's where the people were.

How does this translate into today's culture?

At the inception of SAVN (Salvation Army Vision Network) we gathered some of the most creative minds from the four corners of the Western Territory into a "Creative Caucus." We locked these unfortunate souls in a room and commanded them to create. The Caucus members put their noses to the grindstone and diligently whittled away.

Truthfully, the officers and soldiers who made up the Creative Caucus were in attendance of their own accord. They volunteered their time with the sincere desire to help form a revolutionary new ministry. The original ideas that flowed from that gathering of minds gave us new hope. These folks were outstanding!

At one point, in the midst of the creative chaos, I had a wonderfully random "Eureka!" moment. It came at the hands of our dear friend, Terry Camsey, who stood in front of the group and laid the truth at our feet.

"Throughout history..." he began. "Every government, organization, and movement has followed the same life-cycle." He sauntered over to the white-board and drew an upward sloping line, "Each movement, born of an original idea, quickly slopes up into Revolution. A revolutionary, groundbreaking, new concept that attracts the masses. Hordes of people flock to the movement, clamoring to be a part of radical change. Steam builds and the movement experiences the lion's share of its overall growth during this beginning stage. Until..."

Lifecycle

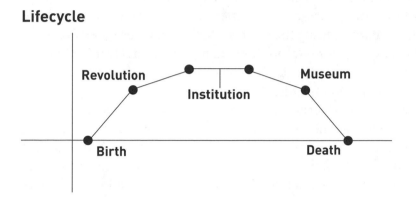

At the top of the sloping "revolution" line, Terry drew a horizontal line and pointed at it. "Institution," he said. "The inevitable plateau. Growth tapers as tradition and protocol bog the system down. The movement stalls."

"As with aerodynamics, a stall is surely followed by the inevitable plunge..." Terry's pen drew a swooping downward line, "Into Museum. In every major movement, this downward spiral marks the beginning-of-the-end. What follows soon after is..." In one final act of penmanship, Terry scrawled the word "DEATH" across the board.

"There is only one way for a movement to cheat death." He continued, "...through REVOLUTION." The group sat silent. "CHANGE is the only known antidote to organizational oblivion. A system must adapt and evolve if it is to survive the long haul. A movement on the verge of death must be reinvented and reborn or it will surely dissolve and fade away."

Terry studied the room. "Now you must ask yourself... Do you want to be involved in The Salvation Army's death? Or do you want to be involved in its rebirth? I believe SAVN to be the first step in our great

Army's movement to reinvent itself. I'm on board because I choose 're-birth.' What you choose is up to you." And with that, Terry took his seat. "Eureka!" I thought. "That's EXACTLY what our Army needs. Rebirth! This man's a genius!" I felt renewed and refreshed; something akin to what Skywalker must have felt while sitting at the knee of Obi-Wan. Time to go out and start the Revolution!

A few months passed. My father ran into Terry at a friend's retirement party. During the Caucus, Terry had taken extensive notes and spent the prior few months organizing them. He told Dad that he had just crossed the last "t" and dotted the last "i" that very day and was going to turn his opus over to SAVN.

Two days later, Terry was Promoted to Glory. It was a tragic blow and great loss to our Army. He was a great man. Though his passing was grievous, it gave me a wonderful peace. The SAVN caucus was the last bit of work that God had for Terry before taking him home. It was an amazing confirmation that God ordained this ministry. Coincidence? You'll never convince me of that.

My friends, though I do not possess the gift of prophecy, I can plainly read the writing on the wall. To quote a grand ole tune, "We're all very grateful to the old folk, who started the Army on its way. But the hope of the Army, yes the hope of the Army, is the young folk of today." We have two choices: We can stick to our patterned traditions and ignore the gathering place of our youth, whereby allowing Satan free reign over their hearts and minds (and likely spell doom for our mission), or we can pick up our armor, meet the Enemy head on, and deliver the Gospel directly to our young people on the digital street corner where they live and socialize.

At SAVN.tv, we strive to develop modern ways of reaching the unsaved amidst a highly distracted culture. We don't claim to have all the answers, but we're doing our best to forge new territory and deliver our message to a generation who lives, breathes, and socializes through the wireless networks. Satan has a strong foothold in the World Wide Web, but he does not have a monopoly. He can be defeated. Our young people can be saved, but we need you, our soldiers, to pick up your swords and fight the good fight. Won't you join us?

Greater Things
"Endless Possibilities"

Carolyn and Jim Knaggs

Jesus said, "Very truly I tell you, whoever believes in me will do the works I have been doing, and they will do even greater things than these, because I am going to the Father" (John 14:12).

Jesus startles us with His pronouncement recorded in John 14, verse 12, when He says about those who believe in Him, they will do the works He has been doing and even greater things. Wow! How can you read that without being amazed at the possibilities? To grasp this extraordinary declaration, we attempt to consider it in three layers of actualization for our life and experience today.

First, we must be true believers. We must be those who "live by faith, not by sight" (2 Corinthians 5:7) and who understand with depth that "without faith it is impossible to please God" (Hebrews 11:6). When we believe, we live with Jesus in our hearts and with Jesus in our minds. That translates not only through what we say, but how we live, walk, and influence others.

We must resemble the Master. It's full time belief with full on engagement. Dietrich Bonhoeffer strengthens the argument about the cost of discipleship being way more than an understanding or a label, but a true love relationship with Jesus. In this we are instructed by His words that remind us, "If you love Me, you keep My commands" (John 14:15 NIV).

Jim and Carolyn Knaggs soldier at the Torrance, California Corps. They first met the Raders while they were conducting evangelistic meetings in Philadelphia. The integrity, intelligence, vision, and veracity exhibited by the Raders have been long-term influences on the Knaggs. Having held command in two territories, their primary role in the salvation war these days, is as evangelists and leaders. They have pioneered SAVN.tv, the online evangelistic initiative of the USA Western Territory, which is reaching the masses with the Gospel.

So the believer is a disciple, giving up one's own way and following the Christ at all costs. It's considerably more than a marginal interest in Christianity.

We see this in practical application when we observe many young people with futures assured by their giftedness, intelligence and discipline that would naturally provide handsomely for their lifestyle, turning to a profession that includes sacrifice, humility and selflessness, for Jesus. Many of these young people find God's leading into ministry roles that send them to places where daily provision is only by faith and the glory of their work is focused not upon themselves, but God.

Lt. Colonel Herb Rader completed his medical studies with a license as a surgeon. In America, he could command a lavish lifestyle and prestige above that of most citizens. He chose instead, with his wife, Lois, to follow God's lead into Salvation Army officership and service in India for many years. Here, they ministered in God's name and great things were accomplished because they are faithful disciples of Jesus. Even upon return home in retirement, they serve God as they are able. Clearly, to know Herb and Lois Rader is to know Christ.

Secondly, by this understanding we can do what Jesus did. Ready to raise the dead? It happens every day in The Salvation Army. In the USA Western Territory alone, we are seeing over 700 men, women and children come alive in Christ every week.

Terry, a 26-year-old man from California, tells me that since he has given his life to Jesus, he's a new man. He thinks, lives and hopes differently than ever before. "My addictions were a slow death, but Jesus has given me life." That is resurrection power. His wife and family are overjoyed with his transformation. They thought he was a "goner." He's not now. He's alive!

Do you remember when Lazarus was resurrected by Jesus, he came out in his grave clothes? Unlike Jesus, whose resurrection was in new shekinah glory, revealing His risen eternity, Lazarus' grave clothes were an indication that his body would absolutely find itself back in a grave eventually. We all will follow Lazarus to a grave, but in Jesus we have victory over death and life forever. The grave does not constrain us. As Leonard Sweet says, the many undertakers of this world were put out of business by the resurrection of Jesus.

As believers, we can prove the realities of a life given to God in the way we bring insight to the spiritually blind, healing to the hurting, and comfort to the lost. These are things that Jesus did and they are miracles even today. We do see God at work in physical healings around us as well. In our family, cancer has taken a few of our loved ones before we wanted them to leave, but God also has healed others among us in His grace and good wisdom.

As a young officer, I witnessed the healing of a dear woman's legs that enabled her to walk without difficulty away from her daily "walkin' sticks." Her witness was always a delight, because God had healed her. Today, she's still walkin' just fine in glory.

How is it then that we can actually find ourselves in the third area of greater things? We believe we can see this as very practical and very real. More than once, Jesus fed thousands of people with no resources of His own. It was always amazing and an undeniable miracle. At least once, there were basketfuls of food left over after the divine provision.

In New York City, The Salvation Army will feed 25,000 people on Thanksgiving alone from resources that are not theirs. The miracle of the many who have given their earnings and their food to The Salvation Army is quite like the boy who gave up his five loaves of bread and two fish to feed so many more. When we recollect what the Army does with the little it receives, we understand it as the provision of God in greater and greater measure. In fact, everything The Salvation Army shares with others has been given to them. It is, undeniably, the hand of God at work.

In recent days, The Salvation Army has engaged in Internet online ministries. They range from streaming live events to recorded Bible studies to video testimonies designed to bring people to faith. The potential outreach is over 2.3 billion people all over the world.

At the time of Jesus, the world population was approximately 231 million people. How many did He speak to? Would we estimate hundreds of thousands? Billy Graham has reportedly preached to over 2.2 billion people in his lifetime and there are more than that online every day hearing the message of God's love from countless sources. The impact in terms of the number of ears receiving the good news in every language is greater with every passing day.

Other believers, like Lt. Colonel Dr. Herb Rader, have skills that go beyond what was even known in Jesus' day. Today, Christian hospitals and medical experts are ministering to people by the hundreds of millions, where faith alone is not efficacious, but remains an essential reality for the expert and the patient.

In all this are we ever greater than Jesus? Of course not, but as He promised, our results would have measurably more impact around the world than in His day.

Jesus' words then were not only a prophecy, but also a promise. By trusting in Him and following His lead, He enables us to do what He did, more and more. When Jesus died and returned to life in glory, it did not signal the end of divine intervention in the lives of His creation. No, He followed up His ascension with the prominent arrival of the Holy Spirit who equips and empowers us to live out this prophetic promise of Jesus with significant increasing impact. Hallelujah!

General Paul Rader and Commissioner Kay Rader both are witnesses to this beautiful plan of God. They too chose to follow God, rather than be tempted to follow a path of earthly wealth and celebrity. Undoubtedly gifted, they would have claimed lofty roles in society and would have been considered most comfortable.

God had a better idea. They followed His lead, saw and participated in the many things that Jesus did all over the world and in many cultures. They concluded their active officership as the international leaders of The Salvation Army, yet with humble hearts and selfless ambition.

While they served in Korea for many years, they returned to the USA for special meetings, often being the primary evangelists in community gatherings. We remember attending one such series of meetings in Philadelphia, where many members of our corps fellowship sought the sanctifying work of the Holy Spirit following

Paul Rader's Spirit-filled message and invitation to pray. We can tell you, miracles happened that day. Our own souls were refreshed and encouraged to renewed life as a result.

What then can we learn from the example of the Raders in the context of faith for greater things? We learn that it starts with God's plan. We then must embrace Jesus to be in the plan. We will see the continuing work of Jesus among us and even greater examples of grace at work every day.

> *God shows us the way.*
> *God calls us to follow.*
> *God continues to apply grace.*
> *God increases the miracles.*
> *Hallelujah!*

The Splitting
(Crisis and Opportunity)

"We live in a world of crisis… The world is on fire and bursting with opportunity at the same time." — General Paul Rader, *Los Angeles Times* interview, July 27, 1994.

> *Now tossed with temptation, then haunted with fears,*
> *My life has been joyless and useless for years;*
> *I feel something better most surely would be*
> *If once thy pure waters, if once thy pure waters,*
> *If once thy pure waters would roll over me.*

Holiness Yesterday And Today

"O Boundless Salvation...The Whole World Redeeming"

William W. Francis

It was a Friday morning that changed the life and ministry of Samuel Logan Brengle. He records that day with the abandoned joy that became a hallmark of his life-long ministry of fervent preaching, prolific writing and passionate living of a life "transformed by the Holy Spirit." In his own words:

> On January 9, 1885, at about nine o'clock in the morning, God sanctified my soul. He gave me such a blessing as I never had dreamed a person could have this side of heaven. It was a heaven of love that came into my heart. I walked out over Boston Common before breakfast weeping for joy and praising God. Oh, how I loved! In that hour I knew Jesus, and I loved Him till my heart would break with love. I loved the sparrows, I loved the dogs, I loved the horses, I loved the little urchins in the streets, I loved the strangers who hurried past me.... I loved the whole world.

This experience would become his life's focus as he taught and admonished believers around the world to seek "the blessing."

Today, 129 years after Brengle's experience, we honor a couple whose lives and ministry were also transformed and empowered by the Holy Spirit — General Paul and Commissioner Kay Rader.

William Francis soldiers at the Orlando, Florida Citadel Corps. Whilst acquainted with the Rader family over a lifetime, his first real contact with this Rader couple was at Asbury Seminary, where Billy was attending. The Raders were there on homeland furlough from Korea in 1967, speaking at TSA Student Fellowship gathering. Since retiring from leadership of the Canada and Bermuda Territory in 2011, Francis continues to preach, teach and serve a chairman emeritus of the Center for Holiness Studies in Florida and member of the Board of Governors for Trinity Western University in Langley, British Columbia. With wife Marilyn he leads annual tours to the Holy Land, including Israel, Egypt, Jordan, Turkey, Greece and Italy.

In his presentation for the Coutts Memorial Lecture Series at Booth College in Sydney, Australia (August 2010), General Rader affirmed:

> The Army has from the start been a holiness movement...the Army is still a vital part of the holiness movement... around the world. Full salvation is emblazoned on our banner of blood and fire, and we mean to keep it billowing.

I will attempt to concisely deal with trends and issues in other churches, followed by a similar look at The Salvation Army.

Trends and Issues in the Global Church

Dr. Kevin Mannoia is professor of ministry and chaplain at Azusa Pacific University and serves as chair of the Wesleyan Holiness Study Project (WHSP). Several members of the WHSP will be well known to Salvationists. They include Dr. Roger J. Green, professor and chair of biblical and theological studies at Gordon College; Dr. Jonathan S. Raymond, president emeritus and senior fellow of Trinity Western University; and Lt.-Colonel Dr. Lyell M. Rader, former ambassador for holiness in the USA Eastern Territory.

In 2004 the WHSP embarked on a two year undertaking to address the substantial topic of the church's mission. In order to achieve the goals of the project, academics and church leaders secured the partnership of the following churches: Church of the Nazarene, Free Methodist Church, The Salvation Army, Church of God, Anderson, Shield of Faith, Brethren in Christ, Evangelical Friends, Church of God in Christ, International Church of the Foursquare Gospel, Christian and Missionary Alliance, and the International Pentecostal Holiness Church.

The WHSP faced head-on the challenging question: "Does the concept of holiness hold any relevance for Christians in the twenty-first century, or is it a theological relic of the past, with little to offer in today's postmodern world?" The overwhelming response to this seminal question is the resolute conclusion that holiness is undeniably relevant in the age in which we live. The biblical doctrine of holiness is essential to following Christ in the twenty-first century.

Kevin Mannoia sagely notes that "…evangelicals are being called to reintegrate social holiness and personal holiness…The principles of integrating social and personal transformation are no longer merely the rhetoric of councils and denominations engaged in turf wars… People who (in the past) attacked each other are now humbly learning from one another." [1]

Mannoia goes on to observe an important, fundamental reality. "The future of the church," he contends, "will be much more defined by missional and theological streams of thought than it will be the institutional structural lines often manifested in sectarian or organizational competition." [2]

Harvey Cox is one of the preeminent theologians in the United States and served as Hollis Research Professor of Divinity at the Harvard Divinity School until his retirement in October 2009. His research and teaching focused on theological developments in world Christianity, including liberation theology and the role of Christianity in Latin America.

In 1965 Harvey Cox's published *The Secular City*. For a book on theology, the volume became immensely popular and influential, selling over one million copies. Cox developed the thesis that the church is primarily a people of faith and action, rather than an institution.

Thirty years later, Harvey Cox reported the phenomenon that is reshaping the church today. In his book *Fire from Heaven*, publish in 1995, Cox observes:

Nearly three decades ago I wrote a book, *The Secular City*, in which I tried to work out a theology for the "post-religious" age that many sociologists had confidently assured us was coming. Since then, however, religion – at least in parts – seems to have gained a new lease on life. Today it is secularity, not spirituality that may be headed for extinction.[3]

Three years after the publication of *Fire from Heaven*, Richard Foster echoes Harvey Cox's heartening assessment:

Today a mighty river of the Spirit is bursting forth from the hearts of women and men, boys and girls. It is a deep river of divine intimacy, a powerful river of holy loving, a dancing river of jubilation in the Spirit, and a broad river of unconditional love for all peoples.[4]

Cox and Foster underscore contemporary reality—the fact that people are hungry for a faith community with a difference. The world longs for a people who really care, love and serve; a people who are different because they know, love and serve a holy God.

Trends and Issues in The Salvation Army

William Booth considered the experience and teaching of holiness as the raison d'être for the Army's existence. In a letter dated October 10, 1886, William Booth confirms:

Bramwell wrote to me last week, saying that it is the experiential realization and definite teaching of the blessing of Holiness that alone can make us different from the other organizations around us. I say Amen. And only this, it seems to me can justify us in having any separate existence at all.

The Army is consciously and actively reemphasizing what William Booth considered our sole justification for "having any separate existence." I include only a partial overview of the Army's refocus on the doctrine and experience of holiness:

General's Consultative Council

The General's Consultative Council, composed of all commissioners stationed at IHQ plus approximately 12 territorial commanders and territorial presidents from around the world, met at Sunbury Court in January 2008 to highlight the subject of the doctrine of holiness in addition to other regular business.

International College for Officers

Recently, my wife and I had the privilege of teaching one of the four segments on holiness at a special session focusing on the doctrine of holiness at the International College of Officers this past November.

International Doctrine Council

The International Doctrine Council has just completed a series of 12 monthly articles in *The Officer* periodical on the subject of holiness. The council is also developing a series of small informative books about what the Army believes — similar in size and format to *The Salvation Army in the Body of Christ* published in 2008.

2010 Theology and Ethics Symposium

The International Doctrine Council hosted the *2010 Theology and Ethics Symposium* at the Sunbury Court Conference Center in England. Approximately 55 delegates from all five zones of the Army world attended this historic event. The symposium theme was *The Doctrine of Sanctification*—with Ephesians 1:4 as the undergirding biblical text: *"For He chose us in Him before the creation of the world to be holy and blameless in His sight."*

Bilateral Dialogue with the World Methodist Conference

The Salvation Army recently concluded bilateral dialogue with the World Methodist Conference, a global association representing 76 denominations in 132 countries with historic and theological Wesleyan roots. The dialogue produced increased mutual understanding and cooperation in many areas, not the least of which has been the re-emphasis on the doctrine of holiness.

Word & Deed

The Salvation Army's theological journal, *Word & Deed*, is co-edited by internationally known Salvationists, Dr. Roger J. Green and Dr. Jonathan S. Raymond. For sixteen years, *Word & Deed* has endeavored to capture contemporary thinking by Salvation Army authors on the subject of holiness. The writings reflect a significant collection of international thinkers. Importantly, the writings affirm our Wesleyan holiness roots and foundations through the contributions of Salvation Army Wesleyan scholars.

Renewed Interest in Brengle Institutes

We have had the privilege of conducting Brengle institutes in all five zones of the Army world. Without question, there exists today a renewed interest in studying and experiencing the blessing of a holy life. Regrettably over the years, I have heard Brengle delegates express what a generation ago would be unimaginable — "I never heard this before!"

Center for Holiness Studies

Lt. Colonel Vern Jewett, divisional commander of the Florida Division in the USA Southern Territory, has recently constructed a state-of-the-art Center for Holiness Studies. The complex was recently dedicated on the grounds of Camp Keystone, just outside of Jacksonville, Florida.

Conclusion

This chapter has been an attempt to succinctly identify the trends, issues and challenges impacting holiness teaching today. It is far from exhaustive. The chapter continues to be written through the lives of those who claim and experience the Lord's never-failing promise: "Now that you have been set free from sin and have become slaves of God, the benefit you reap leads to holiness, and the result is eternal life" (Romans 6:22).

Bibliography

Cox, Harvey. *Fire from Heaven: The Rise of Pentecostal Spirituality and the Reshaping of Religion in the Twenty-first Century*. Reading, MA: Addison-Wesley, 1995.

Foster, Richard. *Streams of Living Water: Celebrating the Great Traditions of Christian Faith*. San Francisco, CA: Harper San Francisco, 1998.

Mannoia, Kevin and Don Thorsen, eds. *The Holiness Manifesto*. Grand Rapids, MI: Wm. B. Eerdmans Publishing, 2008.

Quanstrom, Mark R. *A Century of Holiness Theology: The Doctrine of Entire Sanctification in the Church of the Nazarene 1905-2004*. Kansas City, MO: Beacon Hill Press, 2004.

Rader, Paul. *Reaching the Metaphor of Grace*. A paper presented as part of the Coutts Memorial Lectures at Booth College Sydney, Australia, 2010.

Rightmire, R. David. *Sanctified Sanity: The Life and Teaching of Samuel Logan Brengle*. Alexandria, VA: Crest Books, 2nd ed. 2009.

Snyder, Howard A. *The Radical Wesley and Patterns for Church Renewal*. Downers Grove, IL: InterVarsity Press, 1980.

Devotional Life
"Take Time to be Holy"

Birgitte Brekke

When we use the words devotional life, we refer to our prayer life, our time spent in worship with other people, and the time spent reading the Word of God. How we treasure the moments spent in quietness before the Lord, where we talk to him about thoughts and feelings, worries, sins and temptations, give thanks for all his blessings in our lives, and intercede for our family members, parents, children, friends. How uplifting if we can be sharing fellowship with other believers. How blessed we are when we hear God talk to us through his Word when we read the Bible. Devotional life is all these things, but when presented with this assignment the first words that came to me were these:

> *Ask what thou wilt my devotion to test,*
> *I will surrender the dearest and best.*

These are words from the song in our songbook: "Lord thou are questioning me, Lovest thou me?" The full text reads like this:

> *Lord, thou art questioning:*
> *Lovest thou me?*
> *Yea, Lord, thou knowest, my answer must be;*
> *But since love's value is proved by love's test,*
> *Jesus, I'll give thee the dearest and best.*

Birgitte Brekke-Clifton soldiers at Bromley Corps, London. She first met the Raders when they came for an official visit to Bangladesh, where she and her husband Bo were the command leaders. Their exemplary joint ministry has been an influence on Brekke-Clifton. Currently the international secretary for Europe, she is known as the "Mother" of "Sally Ann", now "OTHERS" founded in Bangladesh, The Salvation Army's Trade not Aid concept.

Chorus
All in my heart, Lord, thou canst read;
Master, thou knowest I love thee indeed.
Ask what thou wilt my devotion to test,
I will surrender the dearest and best.
How couldst thou smile on me if, in my heart,
I were unwilling from treasures to part?
Since my redemption cost thee such a price,
Utmost surrender alone will suffice.

Down at thy feet all my fears I let go,
Back on thy strength all my weakness throw;
Lord, in my life thou shalt have thine own way,
Speak but the word, and thy child will obey.

It is a beautiful song and singing it can be very emotional. No doubt many have sung it and meant every word but each line is a challenge! Yes, Lord I love you, but I also know it is not enough to say it. I most show it by surrendering my will to yours, being obedient to your will for my life.

When reading the opening words of the song, we remember Jesus' conversation with Peter after the resurrection as we read it in John 21: 15–19 (NIV):

When they had finished eating, Jesus said to Simon Peter, "Simon, son of John, do you truly love me more than these?"
"Yes, Lord," he said, "you know that I love you."
Jesus said: "Feed my lambs."
Again Jesus said, "Simon son of John, do you truly love me?"
He answered, "Yes, Lord, you know that I love you."
Jesus said: "Take care of my sheep."
The third time he said to him, "Simon son of John, do you love me?"
Peter was hurt because Jesus asked him the third time, "Do you love me?"
He said, "Lord you know all things; you know that I love you."
Jesus said, "Feed my sheep, I tell you the truth, when you were younger you

dressed yourself and went where you wanted: but when you are old you will stretch out your hands, and someone else will dress you and lead you where you do not want to go."
Jesus said this to indicate the kind of death by which Peter would glorify God. Then he said to him:" Follow me!"

We realize reading this passage of scripture that...*love's value is proved by love's test.* Our devotional life, the time spent in prayer, meditation and worship must lead to other acts of devotion, including those that lead to hardship, suffering and pain and to expressions of love and compassion for others. We picture ourselves in the place of Peter on that day, we hear ourselves answer Jesus' questions, saying, "Yes, Lord you know that I love you" and we hear his words:

"Feed my lambs!"
"Take care of my sheep!"
"Feed my sheep!"
"Follow me!"

"Follow me" for Commissioner Rader meant leaving the church where she was brought up to join The Salvation Army. For Kay and Paul Rader it meant leaving their homeland to work for God in Korea for 22 years and later to take upon them the privilege and the burden of being the world leaders of the Army.

I met the Raders when my first husband, Bo and I were the Command Leaders in Bangladesh. While we were there General and Commissioner Rader visited the Command. It was a visit marked by many unexpected encounters that our world leaders handled with grace.

The final day of their visit was a very busy day. During the morning General and Commissioner Rader visited the "Sally Ann" shop. "Sally Ann" was at the time the Army's emerging fair trade concept, an idea to help women in Bangladesh earn a regular income. At the time I am writing this, "Sally Ann'" has changed its name to "Others", but it is still the same concept, and it still helps hundreds of families earn a regular income. A small shop had opened at headquarters in

Dhaka on September 17, 1997. It sold cards made from handmade paper, embroidered tablecloths, napkins and placemats, leaf baskets and handbags, children's toys, wrought-iron chandeliers and lamp-stands, beautifully crafted furniture. All made locally by hand, giving regular income to families, helping them to look after their own lives, giving dignity, improving their quality of life.

Commissioner Kay Rader had shown a great interest in "Sally Ann," and our visitors took their time. They looked and photographed and asked questions. Commissioner Rader placed the largest order for products to that date. She wanted her official Christmas gifts for all the international women leaders of The Salvation Army to be supplied by "Sally Ann." Commissioner Rader understood the principles guiding this initiative. She knew that this would be the best way of helping people to put bread on the table, that this was about empowering and self-help and she wanted to use her influence to promote trade as a very effective development tool.

Later the same day, our world leaders walked through the slums of Mirpur in Dhaka. Thousands of people live there. The Army has been at work there for many years and operates a medical clinic, a community development project and a corps. Micro-credit was the focus of the visit. Families were given a loan to set up a small business, the loan was repaid in small installments and the money then rolled over to the next family, or a new loan was given so the business could be expanded.

The Raders walked around the slum. Open sewers ran on either side. Heaps of rubbish lay uncollected, attracting flies in the thousands and spreading disease. The world leaders must have seen it all before. Slums are not unique to Dhaka; they exist in many mega cities around the world. Here in Mirpur, The Salvation Army actively sought to address the problems of poverty.

At the beginning of the tour General Rader asked, "How much money do you have available for this scheme?" We told him. "Could you do with an extra $5,000?" he asked. We certainly could. By the end of the tour he had pledged not $5,000 but $30,000. The General's generous donation to the micro credit scheme continues to result in improved lives for some of Dhaka's poor.

"Do you love me?" the Lord asks. When our answer is yes, he tells us to "Feed my lambs!" "Take care of my sheep!" "Feed my sheep!" "Follow me!"

Or as James puts it:

Religion that God our Father accepts as pure and faultless is this: to look after orphans and widows in their distress and to keep oneself from being polluted by the world. (James 1:27, NIV)

Devotional life, our prayer life, reading the Bible, sharing in fellowship with other believers, must lead to other expressions of devotion, often very practical expressions of love and compassion and utmost surrender and obedience to the call of Jesus: "Follow me."

We remember the story of the rich ruler who came to Jesus and asked: "What must I do to inherit eternal life?" Jesus answered: "You know the commandments" and the ruler replied, "I have kept them since I was a boy."

When Jesus heard this, he said to him, "You still lack one thing. Sell everything you have and give to the poor, and you will have treasure in heaven. Then come and follow me." When he heard this he became very sad, because he was a man of great wealth. (Luke 18: 22-23 NIV)

Peter said to him, "We have left all we had to follow you!" "I tell you the truth," Jesus said to them, "no one who has left home or wife or brothers or sisters or parents or children for the sake of the kingdom of God will fail to receive many times as much in this age and, in the age to come, eternal life" (Luke 18:28-30 NIV).

May our devotional life lead us to pray:

> Ask what thou wilt my devotion to test,
> I will surrender the dearest and best.

The Bible

"Break Thou the Bread of Life"

Bramwell Tillsley

The Recovery of Wholeness

It is always a privilege to write or speak on the theme of the Bible. My lifelong passion for the Word has its foundation in two basic truths, namely:

(a) It is the one thing God has promised to bless. "My word will not return to me empty, but will accomplish what I desire and achieve the purpose for which it was sent" (Isaiah 55:11).

(b) The written Word inevitably leads us to Jesus, the Living Word. A beautiful example of this is recorded in Luke 4:16-20:

On the Sabbath day, as was his custom, Jesus went into the synagogue. The scroll of the prophet Isaiah was given him to read. When he finished the reading, "he rolled up the scroll, gave it back to the attendant and sat down." At that point, "the eyes of everyone in the synagogue were fastened on HIM"—not on the scroll.

In an article on "The Recovery of Wholeness" the noted American Quaker Elton Trueblood wrote: "It is unfortunately clear that a great deal of our contemporary religion, including the Christian religion, touches the life of ordinary men and women at distressingly few points." He then added:

Bramwell Tillsley, retired in Toronto, is father of three and grandfather of eight. He was the 18th Chief of the Staff and served in four countries on three continents. The 14th General of The Salvation Army, Tillsley was succeeded by General Paul Rader. He has written four books, including Life in the Spirit and Life More Abundant.

The Christian faith must rediscover its own essential genius, which is the union of the secular and the sacred; the union of matter and spirit; the common and the divine. That religion will have the most meaning that touches common life redemptively at the most points.

The more I read the New Testament, the more convinced I become that Jesus was concerned, not simply with SOUL salvation but with WHOLE salvation. He entered the problems of humanity in a manner that was spiritually creative and socially corrective. The order is significant. Soul salvation is still basic, for Jesus was principally concerned with making new men versus new conditions. We must, however, be aware there is always the danger of creating a false division, for the New Testament emphasis is upon the whole person. When I was a youngster, I sometimes heard the jingle:

> *Salvation Army save my soul,*
> *Send me to heaven in a sugar bowl.*

Though I was highly embarrassed by it all, my concept of "salvation" was little wider than what was indicated in the couplet. To me and many others, salvation was that which saved me from hell and opened the way to heaven.

However, the more I read the New Testament, the more convinced I became that Jesus was concerned, not simply with soul salvation but with whole salvation. Jesus entered the problems of humanity in a manner that was spiritually creative and socially corrective. Soul salvation is still basic, for Jesus was principally concerned with making new men rather than new conditions. The emphasis is always upon the whole person.

Let me illustrate by sharing with you several examples of the use of the noun "soteria" (salvation) and the verb "sozein" (to save)—words translated in various translations by "saved," "healed," "made whole."

Just a glance at the New Testament reveals Jesus concern for the PHYSICAL part of man. Matthew 9:20-26 reports the narrative of the woman with the issue of blood. Mark adds that with all the medical attention she received, she actually grew worse (Mark 5:26). The woman responded, "If I may but touch His garment, I shall be 'whole.'" Here salvation or soteria is linked with the body.

Salvation is also linked with the mind (Luke 8: 26–36). Here we are introduced to the demoniac of Gadara. Chains and fetters were unable to hold him. He was driven into the wilderness by the devil. Then he met with Jesus. From this encounter the record indicates the people saw him, "sitting at the feet of Jesus, clothed and in his right mind" (Luke 8:35). They marveled that, "he that was possessed of the devil was *healed*." Jesus was thus concerned with the body and the mind as well as the spirit. Of course, the salvation does not always provide an immediate cure but it does enable the sufferer to change the suffering to glory. Suffering may color the whole of life, but through this salvation we can choose the color.

This salvation holds us up through the storms of life. The disciples were caught in the storm at sea. They cried out, "Lord SAVE us for we perish" (Matthew 8:25). This was the same cry of Peter when he attempted to walk on the water (Matthew 14:30).

At this point he was not concerned with his sin but with his safety.

Salvation certainly applies to all who are *lost*. "The son of man is come to seek and to save that which was lost" (Luke 19:10). This applies to all who are off course, away from the main stream of life.

In the Sprunt Lectures at Union Theological Seminary, Waldo Beach suggested our world is marked by three basic characteristics: Anomi, Anonymity, and Alienation. Anomi suggests there is no norm for behavior; there are no absolutes or authoritative standards for right and wrong. Anonymity means man has lost his sense of self worth. He is plagued with such questions as, Who Am I? Why am I Here? Where Am I Going? In a computerized age, do I really matter as a person? Alienation implies broken fellowship with God and with man. Perhaps this is why Dr. Carl Jung suggested, "the central neurosis of our time is emptiness." *"So the Son of Man came to seek and to save that which was lost. He came to give us life in all its fullness"(John 10:10).*

Salvation is of course is linked with sin. It was said of Jesus, "He came to save His people from their sins" (Matthew 1:21). To the Christian, this is an ongoing experience. Jesus not only saved us in the past (1 John 1:9) but He saves us now (1 John 1:7). Speaking of salvation, William Booth wrote: "We are a salvation people, this is our specialty; getting saved; keeping saved; getting others saved." To say:

(a) I must sin – denies the foundation of the Christian faith
     (1 John 2:1)
(b) I cannot sin – is to deceive myself (1 John 1:8)
(c) I need not sin – is to state my divine privilege (1 John 3:9)

Finally, the New Testament speaks of "salvation" which is eschatological. This means we begin to enjoy it in the here and now, but its full impact will only be realized when Jesus returns as King. Speaking of this time the writer of Hebrews records: "And unto them that look for Him shall He appear the second time without sin unto salvation" (Hebrews 9:28). The doctrine of the Second Coming preserves the truth that all human history will be consummated in Christ.

God has allowed us to know the secret of His plan and it is this: He purposes in his sovereign will that all human history shall be consummated in Christ; that everything that exists in heaven or earth shall find its perfection and fulfillment in Him. (Ephesians 1:10 Phillips).

Jesus not only gives hope but is our hope. This is a message the world needs to hear. How often we have heard people exclaim: "Where will it all end? "What is the world coming to?" In many instances, people have been conditioned to think along these lines.

Bertrand Russell spoke of, "building one's life on the unshakable foundation of despair." H.G. Wells suggested that man, who began life in a cave, will end it in the diseased ruins of a slum. No wonder there is a mood of uncertainty and even despair. But his is not the message of the New Testament. Again we exclaim: JESUS IS OUR HOPE.

In summary, William Barclay has reminded us that "soteria" or salvation is that which saves a man from all that would ruin him in this life and the life to come. Yes, Jesus was concerned with the total person, that is body, mind and spirit.

Dare we be concerned with anything less?

To General Paul and Commissioner Kay, who for many years have preached "Full Salvation." God has honored your commitment to the Word and we have been the grateful recipients. Thank you, Paul and Kay, for your ministry, which has enriched our lives.

Cracked Pots: Give Us Sincere Hearts

"I Would Be True"

Jonathan Evans

I bring thee, dear Jesus, my all, Nor hold back from thee any part; Obedient to thy
welcome call. I yield thee the whole of my heart.

O speak, O speak while before thee I pray! And, O Lord, just what seemeth thee good
Reveal, and my heart shall obey.

Perverse, stubborn once was my will. My feet ran in self-chosen ways;
Thy pleasure henceforth to fulfill, I'll spend all the rest of my days.

The doubts that have darkened my soul, The shame and the fears that I hate,
O banish, and bid me be whole, A clean heart within me create

O give me a heart that is true, Unspotted and pure in thy sight,
A love that would anything do, A life given up to the fight! (SASB, 422)

The word sincere comes from the Latin, *sincerus*. The prefix *sin*
means without while *cere* means wax. Pottery, as ubiquitous as plastic
in our day, during biblical times was a major trade. Potters who
made imperfect pots with cracks or rough edges would fill in these
imperfections with wax to pass them off as high craftsmanship.

However, careful potters utilizing the finest clay and techniques
would scribe *sincerus* on the bottom to distinguish the vessel as perfect.

Jonathan Evans, who soldiers at Cross Culture Corps in Vancouver, met the Raders at Old Orchard Beach
Camp meetings. He was influenced by their quest for holiness and an obvious investment in souls. He
testifies, "I'm their second generation fruit!" Currently Carla and Jonathan Evans serve as corps leaders
of Cross Culture. They led the War College for eight years and have been recognized as transformational
agents in Vancouver's Downtown Eastside.

To test the quality of the vessel a pot could be held to a flame where the heat and radiance of the fire would melt the wax and expose any imperfection. εἰλικρινής (eilikrinēs) is the Greek word Paul uses in Philippians 1:10 to denote a pure or sincere heart.

*And it is my prayer that your love may abound more and more, with knowledge and all discernment, so that you may approve what is excellent, and so be **pure** and blameless for the day of Christ, filled with the fruit of righteousness that comes through Jesus Christ, to the glory and praise of God. (Philippians 1:9-11, ESV).*

εἰλικρινής connotes that which is examined in the sunlight is determined to be pure and clear. In light of this I propose these questions: Do we Salvationists cultivate a life in the light of Jesus to be pure and blameless? And what difference does this make for us?

A senior officer tells about meeting with his divisional commander at officer's camp. Another obscure and seemingly simple officer happened to walk by. "There is a man in whom there is no deceit!" exclaimed the DC. Intentionally echoing Jesus' one time observation of Nathanael in John's Gospel,[5] the DC was pointing out this seemingly insignificant comrade had something in him that would escape human perceptions. Like Nathanael, this officer was a character who "tells it like it is." Nathanael seems everything but innocent at first, "Can anything good come out of Nazareth?" (John 1:46).[6] Jesus, however, sees something more in him.

Jesus saw Nathanael coming toward him and said of him, "Behold, an Israelite indeed, in whom there is no deceit!" Nathanael said to him, "How do you know me?" Jesus answered him, "Before Philip called you, when you were under the fig tree, I saw you." (John 1:47-48, ESV)

As Nathanael is held up to the glory of Jesus in this Gospel it appears that Jesus has a favorable accommodation for him linked to his examination "under the fig tree." What exactly is the connection? Every religious Hebrew would desire to be described in this way:

Blessed is the one whose transgression is forgiven, whose sin is covered. Blessed is the man against whom the Lord counts no iniquity, and in whose spirit there is no deceit. (Psalm 32:1-2, ESV)

It would be exactly under the fig tree where Nathanael would be seen before Yahweh, reading the Torah. [7] Jesus' word of knowledge highlighting Nathanael's whereabouts during a specific and memorable encounter demonstrates that Jesus himself is God. Nathanael again is encountering Yahweh, "Rabbi, you are the Son of God! You are the King of Israel!" (John 1:49, ESV). Nathanael was invited to "Come and See" (John 1:46) only to find that Jesus had seen him and invites him to greater encounters. "Truly, truly, I say to you, you will see heaven opened, and the angels of God ascending and descending on the Son of Man" (John 1:51). Just as Jacob at Bethel encountered Yahweh where angels "were ascending and descending" (cf. Gen 28:12), Nathanael will discover, "Surely the Lord is in this place, and I did not know it." And "How awesome is this place! This is none other than the house of God, and this is the gate of heaven." (Gen. 28:16-17). Sincerity begins and ends not with moralism but with encountering God. Indeed Jesus is "the gate of heaven," and "the Lamb who takes away the sin of the world!" (John 1:29).

Nathanael's sincere heart is a result of his devotion and encounter with the One who sees all and forgives all. In the light of Jesus our imperfections and sins will be stripped away. In encountering the consuming fire of God our imperfections are clearly seen and we are left as clear, sincere pots: vulnerable, exposed but not burned.

The Salvation Army has a deep tradition of encountering Jesus in humility and personal searching, one that General and Commissioner Rader advanced in the genesis of the Spiritual Life Commission. John Wesley was adamant that the grace of God is continually experienced and transformative in the Christian's life:

And at the same time that we are justified, yea, in that very moment, sanctification begins. In that instant we are born again, born from above, born of the Spirit: there is a real as well as a relative change. We are inwardly renewed by the power of God. We feel "the love of God shed abroad in our heart by the Holy Ghost which is given unto us"; producing love to all mankind, and more especially to the children of God; expelling the love of the world, the love of pleasure, of ease, of honor, of money, together with pride, anger, self-will, and every other evil temper; in a word, changing the earthly, sensual, devilish mind, into "the mind which was in Christ Jesus." [8]

The experience of God's grace is a yearning within to experience and participate in the love of God over pleasures of sin. It is no wonder then that Wesleyans cultivate a strict observance of self-examination. We do not encounter Christ with cowardice and shame but in the light and hope of being renewed into the image of God. Wesley and William Booth encouraged their people to pore over self-examination questions.[9] The pure and blameless life is not one without error, ignorance or fault. Rather, the Christian life is a continual trajectory to experience the love and grace of Christ. The necessary means of grace in pursuit of holiness is drawn into our soldier's covenant:

I will be responsive to the Holy Spirit's work and obedient to His leading in my life, growing in grace through worship, prayer, service and the reading of the Bible. I will make the values of the Kingdom of God and not the values of the world the standard for my life.[10]

By daily setting time for spiritual disciplines soldiers will be held up in the light of Christ. It is in this humble position that we realize our dependence upon his grace and our fellow soldiers. Wesley was sure that salvation worked beyond the individual. He emphasized the communal nature of this journey, "The Gospel of Christ knows of no religion but social; no holiness but social holiness. 'Faith working by love' is the length and breadth and depth and height of Christian perfection." [11] James too emphasizes the discipline of confession, "Therefore, confess your sins to one another and pray for one another, that you may be healed. The prayer of a righteous person has great power as it is working" (James 5:16, ESV). Where is the place for this in our corps meetings and discipleship programs?

After our personal reflection do we have a "holy club" like Wesley, with fellow soldiers who can encourage and pray for us that we may be healed? Proper Christian living incorporates the whole person. Howard Snyder observes that the healing motif broadens a static protestant view of salvation: [12]

> Salvation-as-healing makes it clear that God is intimately concerned with every aspect of our lives; yet, biblically understood, it also makes clear that the healing we most fundamentally need is spiritual: Our relationship to God. Biblically grounded (and as Wesley understood it), the salvation-as-healing motif is no concession to pop psychology; it is an affirmation of who God is, what it means to be created in God's image, and what it takes for that image to be restored in Jesus Christ by the power of the Holy Spirit.[13]

Paul's self-defense in 2 Corinthians 4 stands against Christian allusions of a triumphant Christian over the world. Paul's treasured Gospel capitalizes the gracious nature by which God forgives, sustains and empowers the Christian in the midst of suffering in the world:

> *But we have this treasure in jars of clay, to show that the surpassing power belongs to God and not to us. We are afflicted in every way, but not crushed; perplexed, but not driven to despair; persecuted, but not forsaken; struck down, but not destroyed; always carrying in the body the death of Jesus, so that the life of Jesus may also be manifested in our bodies. For we who live are always being given over to death for Jesus' sake, so that the life of Jesus also may be manifested in our mortal flesh. So death is at work in us, but life in you. (2 Corinthians 4:7-12, ESV)*

We ultimately are cracked pots and God doesn't want us to hide our inadequacies or faults. There is tremendous power that is exclusive to Christianity in the forgiveness of sins and fellowship in the Holy Spirit, which are only evident when the weak fallibility of our mortality is admitted and God's life giving and regenerating power is evident in us. So may we be sincere about our true selves, not hiding our weaknesses but in courageous faith holding our lives up to the light of Christ so that his healing power may be revealed.

TEST FOR SELF-EXAMINATION
(The Salvation Army Orders And Regulations for Soldiers)

1. Am I habitually guilty of any known sin? Do I practice or allow myself in any thought, word, or deed that I know to be wrong?

2. Am I so the master of my bodily appetites as to have no condemnation? Do I allow myself in any indulgence that is injurious to my holiness, growth in knowledge, obedience, and usefulness?

3. Are my thoughts and feelings such that I should not be ashamed to hear them published before God?

4. Does the influence of the world cause me to act, feel, or say things that are unlike Christ?

5. Do my tempers cause me to act, feel or say things that I see afterward are contrary to that love which I ought to bear always to those about me?

6. Am I doing all in my power for the salvation of sinners? Do I feel concern about their danger and pray and work for their salvation as if they were my children?

7. Am I fulfilling the vows I have made to God in my acts of consecration or at the Penitent Form?

8. Is my example in harmony with my profession?

9. Am I conscious of any pride or haughtiness in my manner or bearing?

10. Do I conform to the fashions and customs of this world or do I show that I despise them?

11. Am I in danger of being carried away with worldly desires to be rich or admired?

These are the 22 questions members of John Wesley's *Holy Club* asked themselves each day during their private rations over 200 years ago.[14]

1. Am I consciously or unconsciously creating the impression that I am better than I really am? In other words, am I a hypocrite?

2. Am I honest in all my acts and words, or do I exaggerate?

3. Do I confidentially pass on to another what was told me in confidence?

4. Can I be trusted?

5. Am I a slave to dress, friends, work, or habits?

6. Am I self-conscious, self-pitying, or self-justifying?

7. Did the Bible live in me today?

8. Do I give it time to speak to me every day?

9. Am I enjoying prayer?

10. When did I last speak to someone else about my faith?

11. Do I pray about the money I spend?

12. Do I get to bed on time and get up on time?

13. Do I disobey God in anything?

14. Do I insist upon doing something about which my conscience is uneasy?

15. Am I defeated in any part of my life?

16. Am I jealous, impure, critical, irritable, touchy, or distrustful?

17. How do I spend my spare time?

18. Am I proud?

19. Do I thank God that I am not as other people, especially as the Pharisee who despised the publican?

20. Is there anyone whom I fear, dislike, disown, criticize, hold a resentment toward or disregard? If so what am I doing about it?

21. Do I grumble or complain constantly?

22. Is Christ real to me?

Biblical Leadership For The Kingdom

"How Firm A Foundation"

Roger J. Green

General Paul A. Rader has exemplified biblical leadership throughout his vocation as a Salvation Army officer, and this was evident internationally during his tenure as the General of The Salvation Army. Commissioner Kay F. Rader shared that leadership with him. And because leadership, even in the Church, has the possibility of being misused and misdirected, it is critical that a biblical understanding of leadership for the sake of the Kingdom of God, as modeled by the Raders, be carefully understood. The biblical foundation of leadership begins here. There is only one biblical model for leadership, and that was evident in our Lord. The biblical leader is the servant-leader.

This is so well expressed in the Philippians 2 passage that speaks of Christ emptying himself and taking the form of a servant, an example that some of His disciples did not seem to comprehend. They wanted to know not about servanthood, but who would be greatest in the Kingdom of God, and above all who would sit at his right hand and at his left hand in His Kingdom. Imagine their shock at Jesus' rebuke, "Whoever would be great among you must be your servant, and whoever would be first among you must be slave of all. For the Son of Man also came not to be served but to serve, and to give his life as a ransom for many" (Mark 10:43-45).

Roger Green, who soldiers at the Old Orchard Beach Corps, grew up in the USA Eastern Territory and has known Paul Rader all his life. In Green's words, "What a great model of the Christian life he was/is, and the same could be said for the entire Rader family." The absolute integrity of their leadership and their great preaching stand out among influences. Green's primary focus in the salvation war these days involves writing and research on Army, as well as biblical and theological topics, including opportunities to teach and preach for the Army around the world. Well known for his writings on William and Catherine Booth, and one of the founders of the journal Word & Deed, he realized a 30-year goal in 2012 when the Army held its first International College for Soldiers. That year he was also admitted into the Order of the Founder.

All officers in the Army must have absolute clarity here, following the example of the Raders. Officers will comprehend the message of their Lord only as they recognize the difference between power and authority. They will have power by virtue of their office. However, authority is another matter. Authority is the recognition that power is used to serve the people and not exploit them by way of control. Authority is the recognition of the proper use of power for the sake of the Kingdom. Otherwise, the power is abused, and all authority is lost. The officer who works in this way may still exercise whatever power the office brings, but will have no authority and therefore will not be recognized as a leader in the biblical sense. The Kingdom of God values the servant leader.

"Ignorance of the Bible is ignorance of Christ" St. Jerome

No officer will understand what it means to be a servant leader without a thorough knowledge of the Scriptures, and unconditional love for the Christ of whom the Scriptures bear witness. Officers are expected to know the Scriptures — to teach, preach, and live lives of holiness in accordance both with the laws of Scripture to which we are obedient, and the desire to conform to the image of Christ. St. Jerome has reminded us that "Ignorance of the Scriptures is ignorance of Christ." We simply cannot know the Christ whom we serve or His Kingdom without knowing the Scriptures. The Kingdom of God values servant leaders who are immersed in the Bible, and again General Rader and Commissioner Rader come to mind for their exposition of the biblical text. Preaching has always been at the center of their ministry.

Flowing from knowledge of the Scriptures comes the realization that God has raised up The Salvation Army, that officers in The Salvation Army are committed to that life and ministry, and are committed joyfully. People of the Kingdom have great admiration for Christians who follow their vocations, rejoicing in the Lord who granted them those vocations, and who are constantly envisioning the great possibilities in every situation and every place for the sake of the Kingdom. They admire Christians who love their Lord and the Lord's calling in their lives. This kind of service is possible only when one recognizes that he or she is called to the Army in order to serve the Kingdom of God.

Officers will not serve with joy if they are serving only the Army. They will too quickly see the faults in the movement and become discouraged because their vision does not reach beyond their every-day tasks for the Army. They will forget that they serve the Kingdom of God. When an officer serves the Army in order to bear witness to Christ's Kingdom, then every appointment is a Kingdom appointment where God reigns. The Kingdom of God demands servant leaders who are committed to the Bible and thereby are joyfully serving that Kingdom, and that Kingdom only.

"Once you were not a people but now you are the people of God"
(I Peter 2:10)
But people do not serve the Kingdom as disembodied spirits. All believers serve God within a particular community context with a defined history, a steady tradition and a sure future. Both officers and soldiers are thereby not free from knowing about the Army in which they have enlisted for the sake of the Kingdom. In the Army's Kingdom tradition there are certain theological texts that bring the Scripture and our own doctrines to life. Two such examples are Catherine Booth's *Female Ministry; or Women's Right to Preach the Gospel,* and William Booth's *Purity of Heart.* Of course it is impossible to read that material without both the realization of and the commitment to the fact that we are not a generically Christian movement, but one rooted in the Bible and in the Wesleyan tradition. Commitment to tradition is critical for every officer. General Rader is clear about this, and his election to the office of General was a sign of that commitment.

Transparency of who we are called to be is the only means of survival in a pluralistic society. And as Christian Smith, an internationally recognized sociologist, has noted in one of his books entitled *American Evangelicalism: Embattled and Thriving:*

We might hypothesize that religious groups that are more capable of constructing distinct identity boundaries vis-à-vis out-groups will produce satisfying morally orienting collective identities and will, as a consequence, grow in size and strength. By contrast, religious groups that have difficulty constructing identity distinction in a pluralistic environment will grow relatively weaker (p. 97).

We should not be misled by the title of the book. Although American Evangelicalism constituted the study and research for the book, certain conclusions about religious life generally in a pluralistic society were drawn, including the one quoted. What is critical is the last sentence — without a very clear distinction of who we are as The Salvation Army in the pluralistic environment in which we now live we will grow relatively weaker. Now is the time for officers to be unambiguous about our biblical grounding in a Wesleyan tradition that serves the Church and the world as an Army of God.

I have been pleased to represent the Army in several venues either within the Army (the International Spiritual Life Commission and the International Doctrine Council) or outside of the Army (the Wesleyan Holiness Consortium), and have discovered time and time again that we are highly respected and regarded not because we are trying to copy some other denomination or religious organization, but simply because we are The Salvation Army, and we bring to the table all of the strengths of what it means to be that people set aside for those purposes that bear witness to the Kingdom. The Kingdom demands servant leaders who are committed to the Bible, are joyfully serving the Kingdom of God, and who can speak to the theological grounding of the Army and what the Army is thereby able to give to the Church and the world.

"In honor preferring one another" (Romans 12:10)

Finally, a word about the nature of vocation. Two things come to mind. An ill used phrase in some Christian circles, including occasionally the Army, is the term full-time Christian service, and sometimes the call to officership employs that language. But that belies a biblical and traditional view of the nature of vocation. All Christians are in full-time Christian service for the sake of the Kingdom of God, and all vocations are equally worthy. Officers and soldiers alike need to recognize that great truth. If "In Christ there is neither slave nor free" (Galatians 3:28) then we have biblical justification for such a view. This was one of the battles of the Reformation, and we will do well to stand with Martin Luther on this matter.

Likewise we use the biblical term of vocation rather than the secular term of career. Vocation recognizes a call from God to which we dedicate our lives in full consecration. The term career is the opposite — it signifies a choice that I make for myself and my personally directed goals. It is not an allegiance to a call from above, but from a motivation from within. The Raders have gladly lived out their vocations as Salvation Army officers.

Officers must also revere the call of other officers and in honor prefer one another. Every church polity has built-in pros and cons. And the hierarchical system to which we are committed as an Army has many features to commend it. However, the dark side of the system is that those of higher rank can forget that all vocations are equally worthy and that the further up the hierarchical ladder they are taken the more vigilant they need to be that they are servants of all, and — equally as important—that they honor their fellow officers who are lower in the ranks, and above all—above all—that they honor those who are the soul of the organization, the corps officers. Rank and office does not give an officer privilege. It gives an officer the responsibilities of servanthood, and the opportunity to fulfill the command of Romans 12:10, "in honor preferring one another." As he fulfilled the highest rank in the Army, Paul A. Rader exemplified what it means to prefer others in honor.

The Kingdom of God values officers who are servant leaders, who are committed to the authority of the Scriptures, are joyfully serving the Kingdom of God, who can speak to the theological grounding of the Army and what the Army can contribute to the life of the Church and the world, and who honor one another and their comrade Christians for the vocations that God, by His grace, has granted for the sake of the body.

Conclusion

Here is no easy task. And to be sure, no vocation is more demanding than that of Salvation Army officership. "I bind myself to Him in this solemn covenant, to love and serve Him supremely all my days," so states the officers' covenant. When commissioned as officers, General Rader and Commissioner Rader pledged to do everything possible to fulfill the solemn words of the covenant, and to live out the glorious vision of the Kingdom of God. Nowhere is this more evident than in the continued leadership of the Raders in service to God's Kingdom.

Intertwining Of Family And Faith
"They Shall Come From the East"

Reflections from the Rader Children

To whom much is given much is required. Some may regard this statement as a curse. I regard it as a blessing. This is because of the family in which I was raised. If I were to use a phrase to describe my father over these past 53 years, it would be faith driven resolute consistency. When I was younger and especially during my rebellious teenage years, I saw this as a further reason to rebel. Why do I have to sit at the table for dinner each meal? Why do we have to have devotions around the table and pray when I am so busy? Why do we have to be the last ones out of church on Sunday? Why should I sit through Korean services as well as English services? Now, as an adult, I have experienced the wonderful and humbling gift of hindsight and realized why my family needed faith-driven consistency and traditions in order to survive and ultimately thrive.

We arrived in Korea in 1961. This was a post war Korea, desperate, still defeated after the Korean War, which had scarred South Korea with scathing devastation. Poverty abounded and despite the indomitable spirit of the Korean people, despair was tangible. This was the Korea my parents entered with a 3 year old and a baby. Their challenge was to find their place, to learn the language, to make relationships in a completely Korean community and to make a home in the middle of a fairly dangerous and often desperate environment. Their ultimate challenge was to identify God's role for them in the Salvation Army work in Korea while maintaining their marriage and their family. We did not arrive and move onto a safely guarded compound for missionaries as so many other missionaries did. Instead, we moved into the middle of a Korean neighborhood and we lived just feet away from the Salvation Army headquarters and training school.

Our house had formally been a factory during the Korean War, which meant that it was a long narrow building that consisted of a hallway and four or five rooms that extended off from it. The kitchen was at one end of the hallway and the dining room/living room was at the other end. I remember my mother running down the hallway with the food trying to get it to the table before it got cold. If you stood in the hallway and looked out the windows, you could see into the offices of the headquarters and wave at the officers as they worked. Underneath our home lived the caretaker of the Salvation Army property, whose daughters and sons were my best friends and playmates. I grew up playing in the gutter and around the kimchi pots with the neighborhood children. I learned Korean there and I practiced it with my companions, who were the training school students my parents were teaching. They taught me how to play ping-pong, told me Korean stories, and listened to me babble on in Korean about all of my childhood antics.

One of my first memories of moving into our house in Korea was the bars on the windows. They seemed normal to me then as every building had bars on its windows and every wall had cut glass protruding from the top of the wall as a deterrent for thieves. Breaking into homes was a way of life as poverty and war had left an entire generation of abandoned children and orphans to fend for themselves. In the midst of this, however, I was able to find safety and a haven in my family and its traditions of faith. Both my parents were entirely committed to their work in Korea. Both became fluent in the Korean language. Both found and developed ministries within the context of the Salvation Army work that evolved and expanded over the 22 years they were there. We knew we were living in a home that belonged to The Salvation Army and that we were to treat it with respect. We knew our Land Rover jeep belonged to The Salvation Army and that it was on loan. We knew even if we didn't fully understand at the time that the work our parents did was for The Salvation Army but more than that, we always had an indomitable sense of our parents' lives being lived for God's purposes. This imbued every aspect of our lives as a family.

Because of the chaos of the world outside our house, our parents created a haven of safety, consistency, order and acceptance inside the home. Although at times, I experienced fear growing up in Korea, I knew that I had advocates and dependable sources of help inside my home. Our days began and ended with prayer. Prayers whenever we broke bread, prayers before we went to sleep, prayer before our first days of school or before any challenging events in our lives. I have memories of seeing my mother and father in prayer together and individually in the early morning hours and late at night. My father's office in our home was a sacred place of prayer to me. He had people of prayer and vision on his walls including his uncle Paul Rader, the great radio evangelist and pioneer, William Booth, and his own father, Colonel Lyell Rader, one of the most passionate Christians I have ever known. I would sometimes wander down to see my dad to find him praying over his sermons. Prayer was our foundation. It was our salvation.

My parents also created a haven of family rituals that remain integral parts of our own families and any time we share together as an extended family. Sharing in the sacredness of meals together, daily devotions after the evening meal, time around the table sorting out what was important in life, celebrating Christmas with Advent wreaths and readings, caroling, service to the community were all part of the fabric of our lives together. There were and are so many traditions that make us "family." These have extended now to the grandchildren and great-grandchildren of my parents. Their mission and passion has and always will be doing God's work through The Salvation Army and the many other ways they have found to serve Him. However, none of this work is to be done at the expense of our family. It is something they have fought for my entire life and I thank God for this on a daily basis. They have taught me the art of maintaining and balancing ministry inside and outside the home. To whom much is given much is required. We have been given so much through our parents. Even now, their words to us are those of encouragement, compassion, and support. They love us for who we are and whose we are and this is the greatest gift of legacy we could ever have been given.

Happy Birthday to the most precious Father any person could ever have.

Edie Rader Moon
School wide Drama Director
IB Theatre Arts Instructor
Seoul Foreign School
Seoul, Korea

Looking Like Dad

In recent years I have been told on numerous occasions that I am looking more and more like my dad. This fact was only brought into more clear focus by the recent Asbury University Ambassador magazine cover in which my dad is holding a picture of me in front of him while I hold a picture of my daughter, Brittney, in front of me. The point of the clever cover and article inside the magazine was to highlight the importance of the legacy of a life well lived. We are ultimately remembered by the fruit of our work. Are we not? My father has lived a life that has always had that in mind. I think he knew early on in his life that his sense of mission, his sense of God's purpose for his life and his work ethic would be something that his kids and their kids would inherit and build on in their own lives.

The thing that continues to impress all of us is Dad's continuing sense of mission even as he celebrates his 80th birthday. His enthusiasm, desire to learn and grow and use his considerable talents never seem to wane. Dad has blazed trails his entire work career from his doctoral work at Fuller, his work at THQ in Korea, to the mark he left on the Western Territory, to his groundbreaking years as the General of The Salvation Army, to finally his stint as the president of Asbury College/University. In all of those stops Dad has been a man of vision who had the ability to see the forest from the trees. Yet through it all Dad always knew that leadership was about connecting with people. I have been fortunate enough to come along in his wake at Asbury and continue that missional work of leadership, love and hard work that he demonstrated to me through the years.

The very first volume of the Asburian yearbook summed it up very well as on its pages is written this statement, "Asbury's purpose is to send forth men and women of high education and with knowledge of the deeper things in spiritual life." That job was done well with my dad as he has spent a lifetime demonstrating to those who have come after him what a deeper spiritual life looks like. As my life progresses I pray that I look more and more like my dad each day physically and spiritually.

JP Rader
Education Professor at Asbury University
Women's Volleyball Coach-Asbury University
Wilmore, Kentucky

The Spirit of Worship

Sometimes I want to flee with everything I possess into a few words, seek refuge in them. But there are still no words to shelter me. That is the real problem. I am in search of a haven, yet I must first build it for myself, stone by stone. Everyone seeks a home, a refuge. And I am always in search of a few words. —Etty Hillesum, *An Interrupted Life*

As Salvationists, my parents believed each meal was a sacrament. This interpretation of communion was the reason my dad made sure we had devotions every night after dinner and after breakfast on weekends. After we finished eating and cleared away the dishes, he would pull out the Bible and his devotional book of choice and begin. This was our family ritual, not to be skipped. My older sister usually resisted because she was anxious to return to her studies, my older brother and I squirmed in our seats, but we always deferred to our family tradition and after the devotional, we would end in prayer. Even though it was nerve wracking to be chosen for closing prayer, my brother, sister and I were glad. Extemporaneous prayers can grow quite long. If one of us were picked, we could make sure the prayer was short and sweet. But my parents were vigilant and thorough and after we said Amen!," my dad or my mom usually felt the need for a prayer addendum and would add a few prayer requests of their own. Regardless, we always ended with saying the Lord's Prayer in unison holding hands around the table.

These words now help me remember a time when I was certain of where I was and who I was. Life has carried me to so many places and through so many changes; the Lord's Prayer is now my touchstone. Each phrase grounds me with the certainty that I am not alone and I am loved. When I was growing up, those in the circle around my dinner table, my mom, my dad, my sister and my brother may not have known all of me just as I could not have known them fully, but we were whole and shared an intimate, unique history even before we knew that would be important. Now, regardless of who is sitting next to me in church, I reach out my hand as their sister in Christ and hope they will reciprocate and take mine before we say The Lord's Prayer. If they don't, then I keep my hand extended, palm open to receive God's will as it is in heaven. I become like the child sitting around my dinner table so many years ago who didn't have to understand what was happening, only that I was loved. I hold my hand open for my daily bread and Christ's forgiveness. I bow my head humbled by the years that separate me from that time when life seemed simple, but comforted by the words that have shaped me and remind me of who I am: a child of God, fully known, unconditionally loved. These are the "few words" that are my shelter, the courts where my heart feels most at home to worship, to rest, and to live.

Jennifer Rader Purvis
College Counselor
Hong Kong International School
Hong Kong

More quotes from the children of General Paul and Commissioner Kay:

JP: "They have shown me what a life grounded in faith looks like. Their impact on my own faith journey has been immense. I have, through their example, been able to understand how to integrate Christ into all facets of my life as a father, teacher, coach and husband."

Edie: "There is no end to the influence my parents have had and continue to have on my life. They have shown me what it means to live for God with heart, body and soul. They have instilled in me a desire to live my life with passion, love, vision and God's purpose every single day. Their love for people around the world, for family, and for each other have inspired and shaped my own relationships."

Jennie: "I'd have to add a "me too!" I definitely feel the same about the life of passion, love and vision that Mom and Dad have modeled for us. It wasn't hard for me to understand and experience the unconditional love of Christ. What greater gift is there for a parent to give to their child than to help them experience God's love that is safe and is home no matter where I live in the world? This has influenced every area of my life."

Paul A. Rader And The Salvation Army At Asbury, 1952-2013

"Savior Teach Me Day By Day"

Ed McKinley

The Salvation Army and Asbury University share a long and fruitful connection. This culminated in ways both practical and symbolic in the administration of Paul A. Rader as president of Asbury during 2000-2006. But even an account that centers on Rader's role at Asbury requires at least a brief explanation of the historic context to provide essential color.

The Army and Asbury have much in common. William Booth, the Army founder, and John Wesley Hughes, a Methodist pastor who started Asbury College in Kentucky in 1890, shared Wesleyan theology. Both organizations were committed to winning lost souls to Jesus Christ (salvation) and opening to them great power of His Spirit to fill their hearts with love for Him and for His work (holiness). The "Founder's Song"—*O boundless salvation, deep ocean of love*—could have served as the theme song for both men and their works.

A useful connection between the Army and the college may have been inevitable. It began in a small way in the 1920s after each organization was well established on the American scene.

Converted through an open air meeting in Oakland, California, McKinley has soldiered at corps in all four American territories: Oakland (USW), Madison (USC), Danville (USS), and currently Lexington (USE). When Captain Rader visited Asbury in 1971 to speak at Chapel, McKinley organized a brass band of Army students to meet him at the Blue Grass Airport in the early hours of the morning. He notes: "Their kindness, courtesy and encouragement have been a gift to me over many years. Like all the Salvationists at Asbury, staff and students alike, I was exceptionally pleased and proud to have the former General and Commissioner Rader as the College President and First Lady during 2000-2006." McKinley has written several books on Salvation Army history.

A few Army leaders recognized the value of having educated officers to oversee the growing number of operations that had budgets and responsibilities that called for more preparation than zeal alone could provide. Asbury was a natural fit; it offered recognized college training with an emphasis upon theological principles identical to those of the Army.

The first Salvationist enrolled at Asbury in 1924. When the Southern Territory was created in 1927, the first territorial commander told the new divisional commanders to "visit such colleges as ... Asbury" to see if any of the students could be interested in "the Army's field of service." Samuel Logan Brengle, the Army's apostle of holiness, visited campus as an official guest speaker five times from 1927-1932. One of the first to speak in the new Hughes Auditorium, Brengle told students in November 1929 that "he is sending all his friends this way and advising folks to send their children to Asbury College." [15]

The Depression caused an interruption in Army enrollment, but after 1941 when Andrew S. Miller and Leon Fisher enrolled as freshmen, there was always a Salvationist enrolled at Asbury. The two played a critical role as pioneers in establishing an Army presence on campus. As students, their weekend ministry as "Lee and Andy" made Asbury a by-word in two Army divisions. Their devoted work in applying the ties that bound the two institutions continued after graduation. Miller as an officer was a warm and energetic Asbury supporter in every appointment while Fisher's role as a respected Asbury professor and a popular lay speaker in Army circles rounded the circle of influence. (See Asbury College Registrar's Annual Report 1938-1939, p. 62, Asbury Archives).

Other officers played important roles in this happy development. The vagaries of Army geography placed Asbury College within the Eastern Territory. The Cincinnati divisional headquarters staff recognized the possibilities within easy reach. "Lee and Andy" often visited Cincinnati Citadel and stayed in the home of the officer, Captain David A. Moulton. In 1951 the Divisional Secretary, Major Lyell Rader, had an important part in establishing at Asbury an official branch of the Army's new international club for college students, the

Salvation Army Student Fellowship (SASF). By the mid-1950s, The Salvation Army was an important presence in Asbury campus life.

Lyell Rader in Cincinnati was a noted Army evangelist, tireless proponent of the open-air ministry, a warm advocate for holiness in heart and life and a proponent for higher education for officers. He was also aware that his stewardship of his gifted children required that they go to college, which meant Asbury. All five were famously successful undergraduates: Paul, Class of 1956, Damon, 1954, Jeanne, 1954; Herbert and Lyell, both Class of 1960.

Asbury was a wonderful experience for Paul Rader. He was already an accomplished musician when he arrived at Asbury. He found a group of talented young Army musicians, whom he soon organized as the first regular Student Fellowship Band. As such, Rader prepared them in daily crack-of-dawn rehearsals to play at a musical festival in New York City at the invitation of the Cincinnati division. The band made a notable impression. Erik Leidzen pronounced it a great success. Asbury became respectable in the eyes of some New York officers who had wondered aloud whether any good thing could come from Kentucky, where they apparently imagined that electricity, shoes and safe drinking water were still uncommon wonders.

Except for his preparation of the student band, however, Paul was not actively involved in the ministry programs of the other Army young people. He earned money for college by working on weekends as song leader for local revival and evangelistic services. Otherwise, on weekends he attended the corps in Cincinnati. His parents were on the Army staff there, and he still regarded the city as his home. He and Kay later entered Army officer training from Cincinnati Citadel Corps. Weekend activities aside, however, Paul's life was transformed by his years at Asbury. As an English major, he was inspired by his kindly, committed and learned teachers.

The spiritual environment was consistent and pervasive, constantly sustained by messages in chapel and prayer meetings. Rader soon regarded the campus as "holy ground"—a sense of reverence for the place that never left him. In 1958 while a student at Asbury Seminary, Rader experienced the waves of grace and love that poured out in a spontaneous revival at the college after Professor Lee Fisher spoke in chapel. At Asbury he was given "wider horizons of understanding and grounding in Wesleyan theology." [16]

Asked in a recent interview to recollect his happiest experience at Asbury, Rader replied at once, "Jesus, then Kay!" Paul and Kay Fuller Rader (Class of 1957) met as students at Asbury. They became lifelong partners in love, ministry and leadership. It was at Asbury that Rader and Kay found clarity for their life's work. In the 1950s missionary activities were a major part of student life. Asbury College was at the zenith of its importance as the premier missionary school in the United States. Asbury sent more Methodist missionaries overseas than any other college in the world. All five Raders became officers who served in the international ministry of the Army. Paul obtained two graduate seminary degrees before he and Kay started their formal training as officers. Aside from a two-year interlude in Southern California (during which Paul earned a doctorate in missiology from Fuller Seminary), the Raders served the first twenty-four years of their officership in Korea.

While Paul and Kay served first in distant lands and later in leadership positions of steadily increasing importance, the Army's impact at Asbury developed. A national survey of Army leaders conducted by the college in 1972 confirmed nationwide endorsement of Asbury. The Southern Territorial Commander, William E. Chamberlain, for instance, described himself as "vitally interested in Asbury College and continued good relationships." In 1975 when Chamberlain was National Commander, the Asbury Salvation Army Student Fellowship [SASF] was brought under the official auspices of the Army's National Headquarters.

This recognition was followed in 1983 by another, in brick and mortar: a new SASF Student Center. By the 1980s average annual enrollment of Salvationists was 74. Graduates include Rader, three USA National Commanders, two Canadian (national) commanders, five U.S. territorial commanders, chief secretaries and divisional commanders in three U.S. territories, training college and staff appointments in all U.S. territories, and hundreds of officers in corps and adult rehabilitation work. Five serving Generals made official visits to Asbury. Asbury was often portrayed in complimentary articles in official Army publications. By 2008 Army publications could describe Asbury as the "Salvationist Alma Mater." [17]

For its part, Asbury recognized the value of the Army's endorsement and support for the college. In 1969 Brigadier Andrew Miller was elected as the first Salvationist on the Asbury Board of Trustees, where he served for almost 30 years. There was at least one, and sometimes two, Army officers on the board for the next 43 years. [18]

The most distinguished of all Asbury's Salvationist graduates is Paul Rader. His career is the practical and symbolic culmination of the relationship between the Army and Asbury. He reached the administrative pinnacle of both institutions. Rader was General during 1994-1999. A year later he became the first Salvationist to serve as president of Asbury College, from which he took his "second retirement" in 2006.

Rader came to the presidency with a number of superlatives. His intellectual preparation in the fields of world mission and of international religious issues had no equal among Asbury presidents. No president surpassed Rader in the careful preparation, content and grace of his public messages. Even his memos and printed announcements were precise and elegant. No other Asbury leader had Rader's administrative experience, international exposure and useful relationships with leaders, organizations and institutions across the nation and around the world.

Rader's whole career was based upon the realization that a Christian leader must have the knowledge and experience to know what he was doing and be conditioned by Scripture and prayer to discern and follow God's will in doing it. He understood that a Christian organization with a doctrinal base and venerable traditions that is charged with a clear mission must protect its heritage, while adapting the presentation of that mission to the rapidly-changing society to which that mission will be applied.

Rader recognized that Asbury College faced grave challenges

in the new 21st century, which required a fresh appraisal of this balance. On the one hand, he regarded doctrinal fidelity and a commitment to the central role of liberal arts in the curriculum as fundamental and nonnegotiable. On the other hand, Rader shared with the founders of both Army and Asbury that adaption of methods to meet changing conditions cannot be avoided, and should not be postponed, lest the moment be lost. Writing in 2000, Rader quoted approvingly from an 1886 memo from William Booth to officers in India, in which the first General informed the Army missionaries that they were "not bound by any stereotyped or antiquated notions." However things had been done in the past, or were being done now, "need not be any rule to you, unless you can see it is calculated to gain the end you have in view."[19]

The practical achievements of Paul Rader's administration at Asbury reflect his balance of foundation and adaptability. He reaffirmed the role of the liberal arts as the center of the academic program with striking eloquence.

Liberal arts in a Christ-centered environment holds the promise of expanding your awareness of the wonder of the created universe. It exposes you to the great minds and the best in literary expression. You explore the world of grand ideas, of aesthetic experience and human potential.[20]

Happily for the school, retirement did not close Paul Rader's role at Asbury University (the name changed in 2011). Recognizing the great success and even greater potential of Asbury's nationally-recognized communication arts program, Rader and Commissioner John Busby guided a proposal through Army administration that led to an equal financial contribution from the four Army territories towards the new communications arts building on campus. The facility, which was dedicated in 2011, is named for Commissioner Andrew S. Miller, in tribute to one of Asbury's most devoted and influential officer friends. The Army's total contribution to the new facility was substantial. It was another historic first. The Army does not ordinarily contribute to other non-profit organizations. This was achieved because of the friendly support of the four territorial commanders, which reflected their recognition that Asbury's value to the Army was national in scope.

As the person most qualified to value the future relationship between the Army and Asbury, Paul Rader is comforted by the school's continued success both in confirming the young Salvationist's sense of vocation and in providing effective preparation for carrying it out. His successor, Asbury President Dr. Sandra Gray, (2007), is delighted by the school's beneficial ties to the Army. The latest proof came in October 2013, when the Eastern Territory and Asbury University signed "an historic memorandum of understanding." By its terms, all officers in the territory will be enabled to take courses at Asbury, leading to a "custom-built" bachelor's degree in "ministry management with an emphasis on nonprofit administration." President Gray allowed that it was only "natural that we would launch this initiative with a long-term friend." General Rader sent the cadets a strong endorsement of the new program via SKYPE, using the same terms he used to recall his own college days. This was the latest but is surely not the last service the General offers to his *alma mater*. [21]

Spiritual Leadership
"Lead On O King"

Eva Burrows

I was delighted to accept the invitation to participate in this festschrift. For many years I have admired the Spirit-empowered leadership of Paul Rader, and his spiritual stature.

Accountability

Accountability is a significant word in use these days — in politics, business, social responsibility, etc. A modern word, it is not seen in most of the new Bible translations where it is expressed in the old Bible phrase "faithful stewardship." Accountability is an important quality of the character and activity of all Christian leaders. Jesus often spoke about it, particularly in His parables such as the parable of the talents, or of the sheep and the goats, or the rich foolish farmer.

The leader's *first accountability is to God,* for the gifts he has been given and the opportunities for service and leadership. I once told General Arnold Brown that he was "a ten talent officer." He said, "That is terrifying. Just think how inadequate my answers will be when I stand before the judgment seat of Christ." The words of Christ were well understood by him – *From everyone who has been given much, much will be demanded* (Luke 12:48).

Eva Burrows soldiers at Melbourne Project 614 Corps, Australia Southern Territory. In her words, "I first met Paul when he was a delegate at the Training Principals' Conference in early 1974. It was held at the International College for Officers in London. I was the principal of the College. I have enjoyed and profited from every contact with them, including the time when Paul was the General. I had the privilege, at their invitation, of conducting their installation as the General and world leader of Women's Ministries in the Westminster Hall in London. What impressed me most about Paul was his commitment to world mission, to The Salvation Army's ethos, and his spiritual depth and authority." Burrows, who has served on four continents, is now an active recruiting sergeant in her corps and continues to fight, inspire and influence Christians around the world. And she was the 13th General of The Salvation Army.

A spiritual leader is also *accountable to his church,* in our case The Salvation Army, which has given him training, a place of service and the privileges of leadership. The church has a right to call us to account for the way we are using those privileges and opportunities in leadership.

A spiritual leader is also *accountable to himself,* how he is using this one life he has to live, making the best of his time and talents, his motivation, learning to know himself and living the holy life which enhances his leadership and gives honor to God. In Acts 20:28 Paul reminds the leaders of the church at Ephesus to "Keep watch over yourselves" before advising them to "Keep watch over your flock."

I have observed Paul Rader and his leadership over many years and seen the strength of his accountability in all three aspects mentioned above. That is why he has been able to stand tall before his people, confident in the Lord, with no need for pretentiousness or platform pose. When he lectured or preached the listener felt that Paul was assured that he was giving an account to God of what God wanted him to say.

An effective spiritual leader knows his own worth, his own strengths and weaknesses. This gives an inner security that enables him to free others on his team to become their best. Helping them to discover, dedicate and deploy their gifts for the Kingdom and not for themselves. In one of his books, General John Larsson relates a Jewish parable which states that when we go to stand before the judgment seat of God, He will not ask: "Why weren't you a Moses?" He will ask, "Why weren't you yourself?"

Culturally Sensitive

We are living in a world that is becoming increasingly culturally diverse, and leaders of the future need to become more culturally sensitive. This is something that has impressed me about Paul Rader's leadership, whether in Korea, America or worldwide. In the early 1970's when he was a young major, I heard him give a lecture on contextualization, when the word was new in theological and missiological circles. He emphasized the need to communicate the message of truth in its cultural setting, and set the standards of leadership with an understanding of the cultural context in which the people live.

The Apostle Paul worked effectively in many cultures. While refusing to dilute the core of his message "to please men," he would go to any lengths to avoid giving offense or putting needless difficulties in the way of people's understanding of and response to the Gospel: *To the Jews I became a Jew, to the Gentiles I became a Gentile, to the weak I became weak...I have become all things to all men, that by all means I may save some* (1 Corinthians 9:19.)

Kay and Paul were partners in this aspect of spiritual leadership. For example, in Korea they studied the language and were quite at home talking to people, both Salvationists and non-Christians, comfortably in their mother tongue. This is one of the finest ways of learning to understand your people. Not an easy task when having to be done in your spare time!

The Apostle Paul didn't throw truth at his listeners. He went out of his way to get alongside them, to start thinking from where they were, whether in Athens or Rome or Jerusalem. He avoided saying or doing anything that would prejudice them against the Gospel or against the ministry for Jesus Christ. He sought to be relevant to the context of his hearers and other leaders with whom he worked.

I see this as a key to the ministry of the Christian church today—such contextualization not only with people from other nations and cultures, but also with the sub-cultures that we need to understand. For example, in Western countries there are the sub-cultures of the pop world of modern youth, the X and Y generations, the New Agers, the post-moderns. Each has a language and a set of values of its own. A spiritual leader needs to come to grips with this so that, not just his preaching, but also his strategies and ministry objectives, reflect this awareness and cultural sensitivity.

Servanthood

The role of a servant is the hallmark of a spiritual leader. It is the biblical model. Jesus Himself defined leadership as service. When on the way to Jerusalem in conversation with the self-seeking sons of Zebedee, He said that the one who would be powerful in His Kingdom must be servant of all. Then He went on to expand His teaching with the whole group of disciples by using Himself as an example — *Even the Son of Man did not come to be served but to serve, and to give His life as a ransom for many* (Mark 10: 35 – 45).

A most powerful demonstration of servanthood was in the Upper Room on the night before His sacrificial death on Calvary, when Jesus washed the disciples' dirty feet with His hands—the hands of God. *You call me Teacher and Lord and rightly so. I have set you an example that you should do as I have done to you* (John 13:1–17). He calls all spiritual leaders to that kind of servant-love, where no task is too humble, no person too low that they cannot stoop to serve them. He makes clear that it will involve suffering and pain, but to suffer for Christ is a privilege not a penalty.

I read of the principal of a theological college who told the students about to be ordained that they would find in their room a farewell gift. To their surprise each received an envelope containing a piece of toweling with a note, "Keep this to remember that you go out as servants, for Christ's sake."

Being a servant goes against the human grain. We don't even like the word, and avoid using it in the secular world. We invent euphemisms to over-rate the name of some inconsequential jobs. Power is generally equated with position and status, but Jesus turned that power-scale on its head by equating power with love. Not love of power, but the power of love. Because of His love, Jesus had power *with* people, rather than power *over* people. The truest expression of love for Christ as spiritual leaders is to be His servant, and the servant of His people.

Being a servant leader does not mean that you abdicate responsibility. Jesus the servant nevertheless knew that the Father had put all things under His power (John 13:3). He had a strong sense of calling and destiny, but He used it to serve rather than to "Lord it over others." God approved and honored His servanthood, for in the first Servant Song of the prophet Isaiah, God speaks: *Here is my servant, my chosen one…In whom I delight* (Isaiah 42:1). Truly God still delights in the servant leaders of His people.

This is a quality seen in Paul Rader's character and leadership. Despite his very impressive line of academic achievements, including a doctor of missiology, and other great gifts and abilities, he remains an unassuming man, even modestly reserved at times, and never ostentatious. Humbly indifferent to praise or acclaim, always giving honor to God, the giver of these gifts, Kay Rader was his great strength in this preparation for leadership when she held a corps appointment so that he could be free to undertake his doctorate in missiology in Los Angeles. Paul ensured her place in their shared servanthood ministry.

It often happens that when a person rises in position and status, even in the church, the tendency to pride increases. If not checked that attitude will disqualify the person in God's eyes for future responsibility in His service. When I was the leader of The Salvation Army in Scotland, the Salvationists often used a phrase in their prayers, *"Hide the Commissioner behind the cross."* I reflected on it often. If a leader is hidden behind the cross, he will view the world and the mission through the eyes of the suffering Servant, and that is a great antidote to pride.

Prophetic Ministry

Many people tend to forget that the word prophet has two meanings — one as a *foreteller* under God's directions of what is to come in the future, such as the inimitable prophet Isaiah who prophesied the coming of the suffering servant Messiah hundreds of years before Jesus' birth. A prophet is also a *forthteller,* challenging his hearers about God's will and purpose for their lives, and showing where they have fallen short of God's requirements. A good example is the prophet Jeremiah who, despite great persecution, fearlessly proclaimed God's word to bring the people of Israel to repentance.

It is quite common when The Salvation Army holds a High Council to elect a new General as world leader, that Salvationists discuss the qualities and type of spiritual leader they are hoping for. Invariably someone will say, "What we need is a prophetic General." What do they mean? They want a leader with strong convictions able to speak boldly about the faith and the practice of his hearers. Even fearlessly proclaiming what God has revealed to him for the whole church, seeking to awaken them to the requirement of the Lord to be His Light to the world. He challenges them to reflect on whether the church is being true to His foundational purpose. Nor should they lose the vision by merely maintaining the status quo, and being complacent and even content with things as they are. Even calling the church to repentance and the quality of holy living, which will open a new future of power in God's service.

I believe this was a strong point in Paul Rader's spiritual leadership. During my years as General, I watched him making decisions from the strong moral imperative he held, not just from Salvation Army policies and procedures. In the many lectures he gave, I heard or read his fearless declarations of what God was requiring in truth, justice and grace — what God was calling Salvationists to be and to do and to fulfill their place in the Kingdom of God.

Passionately Mission Motivated

Mission now covers a wide area of ministry — evangelism, social justice, social practice and community involvement. A spiritual leader must have these in the forefront of his strategic planning and action. So he must focus his attention on The Great Commission — *Go into all the world and make all* nations *my disciples* (Matthew 28:18-19) and the Great Commandment — *Love the Lord your God with your heart, and soul and mind and strength, and love your neighbor as you love yourself* (Matthew 22:34-40). The leader's great ambition in evangelism is to carry out the mission statement of Jesus Christ who came *to seek and save the lost.* He works creatively to discover the most effective ways of winning for Christ those who have never believed before, and those who have turned away because of disillusionment and disenchantment with the church. This will involve him in creative methods of evangelism and in the adaptation of the means of communicating the Gospel.

Jesus said, *If I be lifted up, I will draw all people to myself.* Simply stated the Gospel IS Jesus Christ, who alone can give true life, offer forgiveness, share our sufferings and meet our needs. Jesus has always been an attraction, and spiritual leaders must see that their Gospel message is centered on Christ.

The ministry of social justice and social action is a powerful calling for The Salvation Army when we demonstrate that Christ is alive by sharing the hurts, the heartaches and needs of those about us. John says it so well. *My children, love must not be a matter of words or talk. It must be genuine and show itself in action* (1 John 3:18). Jesus demonstrated the meaning of caring involvement. He was concerned with the whole person. He opened the eyes of the blind, the physically blind and the spiritually blind. He announced good news to the poor, the economically poor as well as the spiritually poor. He fed the hungry. He cared for those alienated from society.

Although He was the greatest teacher the world has ever known, he was not a word merchant. He had a powerful practical ministry and that is what he has bequeathed to The Salvation Army. Again and again in the Gospel stories Jesus condemns the person who refuses to be involved. Spiritual leaders of the church cannot ignore this charge, this challenge, from Jesus Christ. This is not some so-called "social Gospel." This is the expression of the true Gospel that must engage the hearts and minds of spiritual leaders, and influence their actions.

As a student of missiology, Paul Rader was very mission-minded, inspiring others to ventures of soul saving, evangelistic efforts. He also understood Christ's bias to the poor, and stimulated endeavors that involved his people in social justice endeavors and schemes for social action.

A Strong Prayer Life

The power behind a strong spiritual leader is his relationship with God, and this is maintained and developed through his personal, devotional prayer life. If there is one area in which a leader should be ahead of his followers, it is in his prayer life. Daniel is an example of such a leader whose prayer life was characterized by a holy awareness of God. To him, God was supreme over all the earth, full of wisdom and mighty power. So Daniel habitually set aside times for prayer no matter what the circumstances, or what the pressures, so that he could plead for God's mercy, grace and forgiveness. Today's spiritual leaders are often, metaphorically speaking, in the lions' den, but, as with Daniel, prayer will shut the lions' mouths.

There can be no substitute for prayer, not even ardent devotion to God's Word and work, or a holy enthusiasm for mission. Nothing can take the place of prayer. Bill Hybels, that frenetically active world-famous Christian leader, appropriately named one of his books, *"Too Busy NOT to Pray."*

Henri Nouwen in *The Way of the Heart* writes that in prayer and solitude we get rid of the scaffolding of our lives. Scaffolding? That is the artificial supports that hold us up, and give us an unreal sense of our own importance and ability. Through prayer the scaffolding falls down, and we know with a new realism that our dependence is on God.

Paul Rader's father, Lt. Colonel Lyell Rader, was known as a great prayer warrior, so Paul grew up in an environment of prayer. He imbibed this holy atmosphere and early understood the words of Jesus, *watch and pray,* in his own prayer life. Paul and Kay served more than two decades in Korea. The dynamic prayer power of The Salvation Army and its people is well documented around the world. That would have had a strong influence on the development of Paul and Kay's practice of prayer. They were certainly partners in their prayer life both for themselves and for their people. I recall reading about the period of prayer in the Holy Spirit when Paul and his fellow leaders claimed goals for the territory right through to the year 2008, when the Army would celebrate its centenary. And how wonderfully God answered those prayers.

The Pastoral Role

Spiritual leaders have a genuine concern for the people they lead. This is their pastoral role as shepherds of the flock of God, which Jesus exemplified as the Good Shepherd, and explained in His teaching.

Shepherd is a biblical term for a leader who empowers others, helping them develop, trusting them with responsibility, testing their commitment. He invests his life in his people and produces leaders like himself.

TSUNAMI OF THE SPIRIT

A spiritual leader respects the people he leads. He works with whatever people are available; never despising them, no matter how weak they may be. He does not defend himself by blaming them for his own failures. The disciples were not an impressive bunch, but Jesus never disdained them. He grieved over them, felt disappointed in them and was deserted by them, but He never disparaged them. Of God's ideal servant it is said, *He will not crush those who are weak, nor quench the smallest hope (Isaiah 42:4).*

Neither is a leader afraid of those he leads. Moses showed great generosity of spirit toward Eldad and Medad *(Numbers 11:28-29)*, even when Joshua wanted them stopped from prophesying in apparent competition with Moses. It was a beautiful lesson in gracious leadership. A spiritual leader does not force out strong men under him, and replace them with weak, more malleable people whom he can easily influence. These are the people we call "Yes men" whose praise and adulation can never be sound advice. The biblical example of "Yes Men" were the false prophets. The true prophet Nathan, with his personal challenge and wise criticism of King David's sinfulness, was David's most valuable adviser.

An effective spiritual leader helps to build a team spirit. Shepherd leadership is relational, not an authoritarian command requiring blind obedience. The Shepherd cares for his people and wants to work alongside them. The term used in the Salvation Army these days is *Consultative Leadership* — leaders working together, and Paul and Kay fully modeled this form of a united group, seeking consensus through the Holy Spirit with no aggressive competitive attitudes nor pulling of rank.

Holy Spirit-Empowered Leadership

More than ever before leaders of the church must be Holy Spirit-empowered men and women. We are in an age when the doctrine of the Holy Spirit has come out of the mystic shadows and into the glorious light of experience. The Holy Spirit need no longer be an enigma, a ghostly mystery to Christians, for we now see Him to be God at work in the world and God at work in you and me.

He is *indispensable* in the growth of the church, and all leaders of the church need to be Spirit-filled and Spirit-directed. I heard a Salvationist say, "There's no point in speaking about the existence of the Holy Spirit, if you have no experience of Him." It is essential for leaders to have a vital experience of the Holy Spirit, for He enables them to lead in ways that would otherwise seem impossible.

The Holy Spirit is God's agent for change in our personal lives and also for the church. Through His conviction He brought us to a transformed change in our lives as we were led to faith in Christ. Then that change continued through the Spirit's sanctifying power, and we became conformed to the image of Christ. He changes our character and motivation as He develops in us the fruit of the Spirit. (The whole of chapter 8 of The Epistle to the Romans, and Galatians 5: 22).

He is God's agent for unity and growth in the church. After all, the Holy Spirit brought the church into being at Pentecost. In Ephesians we see the power of the Holy Spirit reconciling Jewish and Gentile believers. *By one Spirit they were baptized into one body.* The members served one another in love, in a bond of unity, worship and service. Spirit-filled leaders build Spirit-filled churches, and Spirit-filled churches flourish to the glory of God.

When Jesus spoke to His small group of disciples in the Upper Room before His death on the cross, He gave them some inspiring teaching about the Holy Spirit whom He would send to them, and promised, *I am sending you ANOTHER counselor to help you and to be with you forever (John 14:16).* It is through the personal counseling of the Holy Spirit that spiritual leaders develop power and authority and Kingdom growth.

I believe Paul Rader was a Spirit-led leader. Intertwined throughout his preaching and teaching the Holy Spirit was a formidable presence. The Word and the Spirit were central to all he planned and brought into action in leadership whether in Korea or America or in the worldwide Salvation Army. It was obvious that to him personally the Holy Spirit was indispensable in his leadership.

On his 80th birthday, may God be pleased to bless him abundantly, and Kay, his partner in ministry and spiritual leadership.

The Amplification
(Risk and Possibility)

"Jesus is looking for risk takers, dare devils who push the limits of possibility... in order to be available for the doing of his sometimes dangerous will."
— General Paul Rader (Ret.), Western Youth Institute, August 7, 2013.

The tide is now flowing, I'm touching the wave,
I hear the loud call of the Mighty to Save;
My faith's growing bolder, delivered I'll be;
I plunge 'neath the waters, I plunge 'neath the waters,
I plunge 'neath the waters they roll over me.

Come Roll Over Me

Holy Boldness!

Editorial Preamble

From a distance (as we never served together, unfortunately), I have long admired Bill Miller, his unorthodox, no nonsense radical style and spirit, with an ample supply of genuineness thrown alongside. Some have cast me as a radical along the way, but I must confess to being a neophyte when compared to Miller... and, being honest, a bit of spiritual envy too. As a Jesus inspired risk taker, my courage and bravery pales by comparison.

Read history, and you will find that the brilliance of the Army, during its formative years, was fueled by a cadre of like minded spirits, unconventional, avant-garde, maverick geniuses. And that same spirit needs to be accepted, applauded, and modeled today, the Raders being pacesetters in this respect.

For this reason, I wanted only one person to write the chapter on Holy Boldness; (there was no Plan B), and to make it quintessentially Envoy Bill Miller. I was not to be disappointed. In fact, let's subtitle the following, "A Gigantantormous Miller Magnum Opus."

Joe Noland

Holy Boldness!

"He Who Would Valiant Be"

Bill Miller

Both General Paul and General Kay Rader have been great examples to me, not only as Salvationists, but they have been mentors. They have cared about me in little ways that normal people have not. I could really give a rip whether they were General of The Salvation Army, or president of Asbury University, or the CEO of Chevrolet; what I care is how people treat you one on one when the limelight's not on and the crowds not around and it's not some kind of show.

The Raders are real. And they have shown, both of them, that they are Brave. How many people that you know could go and lead an organization in a foreign country?

And the Raders have gone to areas all over the world that we would be scared to death of going to. I think I'm brave because I've worked at ARC and Harbor Light for 20+ years in some of the roughest areas of the U.S., but that is nothing in comparison to what the Raders have done.

They have gone and served wherever the Lord has called them—with no griping, no complaining, unlike me and so many others who want to pick and choose where they go. So the word "brave" comes back to me, again and again, when I think of the Raders.

Bill Miller soldiers at the Minneapolis Harbor Light, where, as the lead officer, he preaches most Sundays. He knew the Raders as a young kid in Kearney, New Jersey. Miller reflects: "They always took time to thank me for being who I was and always even when they were big shots go out of their way to make sure my heart was right. They have also showed me that you can be as smart as Stephen Hawking and yet come down and be humble enough to treat everyone as equals." Miller has a "huge and growing" corps where "God has our altars filled every day." His ambition is to be "in the deepest, darkest, places so that I can bring some light. I am a nobody trying to save everybody."

```
B R A V E
O A C I X
L D T R A
D I I T M
  C V U P
  A E O L
  L   U E
      S
```

B: In order to be an effective leader or an effective Christian, you have to have a holy boldness about you; now I don't mean a rude boldness, but a person who is willing to go places that are uncomfortable, to situations that are scary, to people who may not understand you, without fear, because you know that Jesus has your back.

Now the Raders have depicted holy boldness throughout their whole lives. Going on mission trips, going to appointments that weren't glamorous, and to others that were way too glamorous, without fear, because they knew Jesus would go with them anywhere. Wherever they were, they stood out as beacons of Salvationism and more importantly, of Christiandom. They are both bold.

R: R stands for Radical. Radical being that they have both been leaders in social movements and in their careers.

Kay has demonstrated an unflinching desire to do missionary and ministry work, has led a charge to invade closed regions with the Gospel of the Lord Jesus Christ, and engaged in more social campaigns than you can shake a stick at.

And Paul, with his "gigantantormous" brain and heart, leading the charge in so many movements, including being the General of this Army and being the president of Asbury University.

You talk radical—radical means you're not like everyone else. You're willing to risk your life, you're willing to risk everything, you're willing to risk whatever to save whosoever.

Now radical is probably not a word that most people would ascribe to the Raders, but in my mind they are perfect examples of what William Booth wanted, and what Jesus wanted—difference-makers, not cookie-cutter people; they are unique, they are radical, to their very essence.

A: I really don't need to write anything here. Any of you who know them or have heard about them know that they are active in every facet of life. They're in better shape than most guys my age. They're active in humanitarian organizations, in The Salvation Army...I don't think there's been anybody more active in their careers than these two Jesus fanatics.

V: As far as the holiness movement, there are no two better examples than the Raders. They have clean hearts, clean hands, and a spotless reputation. I mean, as far as being brave, in order to go into places and do things no man or no woman has done before, you have to have a virtuous heart.

You have to show that you are real, and that you are more than just talk; you have to lead a life that shows others plain and clear that you're not doing this for your own advancement, but you're doing it to help others. If you're real and you're virtuous, people will follow you and will have their hearts changed by your virtuous and brave heart.

E: Kay wraps up the idea of being brave—you have to be an example. You have to be able to stand up where others shrink away, you have to be able to speak the truth where others water it down, people have to see you willing and able to go into the toughest places and not act like you're something special but be normal and real. Do you want to see brave? Look at the Raders' lives. Look at their works. Look at their words. And look at their hearts. That's being brave. That's holy boldness! They are people I would follow into the gates of hell.

Examples To Follow

"Jesus, Savior, Pilot Me"

Janet Munn

"Follow my example, as I follow the example of Christ, wrote the Apostle Paul to the believers in Corinth (1 Corinthians 11:1).

It was through the preaching of General Paul Rader that this verse was first quickened to my heart. It was through the lives of Kay and Paul Rader that I have done exactly that, for nearly three decades. Their example of spiritual depth, discipline and devotion, has been a source of inspiration to me ever since I first came to know them. At that time I was a cadet and they were the leaders of the School for Officers' Training for The Salvation Army, USA Eastern Territory.

What do we look for in those we consider to be examples of spiritual vitality and vibrancy? Fidelity? Consistency? Humility? Creativity? Zeal? Eagerness to learn? Able to teach? All of these qualities and more, I have seen in the Raders.

Those in Christian leadership can leave behind all kinds of leadership legacies, for example, great buildings or effective programs. Yet one of the many lasting influences in The Salvation Army, from the leadership of Paul and Kay Rader, came from their season as the international leaders of The Salvation Army.

During that time they established the international spiritual life commission, which offered a renewed emphasis on the spiritual life of Salvationists. In convening the commission in 1996, General Paul Rader wrote:

Janet Munn is currently invested in helping to train up a generation of Blood and Fire leaders in the Australia Eastern Territory as training principal. She first met the Raders when they were her training principals in USA Eastern Territory. Since then, their lives of steadfast devotion to Christ and His mission in and for the world, to the Scriptures, and to prayer have influenced her. Munn is known for her commitment to Scripture, extraordinary prayer (24/7, fasting...), discipleship through small groups, helping people to grow in their spiritual lives in Christ, discipling young people, and mentoring and developing women in leadership.

Simply put, it is time for us to take more seriously issues related to our inner life. We owe it to our people. It is essential to maintaining the engine of commitment and passion. Our mission is energized by our spirituality...Further, the Evangelical Church, and the Army within it, is more embattled by powerful spiritual forces than ever before. Our people need to be armored against the enemy of their souls.

The international spiritual life commission report included several recommendations for further spiritual life emphasis throughout the international Salvation Army. From the commission's recommendations came the establishment of the Center for Spiritual Life Development (CSLD) in July 2008—a ministry of the international Salvation Army. This center's mission is to facilitate the spiritual lives of Salvationists, which it has been doing, since its inception five years ago. This now includes a non-stop prayer initiative, the Global Call to 24/7 Prayer: A Day and Night Cry for Justice, which is happening around the world, and around the clock in more than fifty territories, with hundreds of Salvation Army centers participating. Further, many territories are giving greater emphasis to nurture of the spiritual life by means of appointing officers to that work specifically, by renewed vigor in disciple making, small groups, mentoring, and spiritual disciplines. All of these, and more, are resourced and supported by the international Center for Spiritual Life Development. All of this is directly related to the spiritual leadership and legacy of Paul and Kay Rader.

If General Rader's words quoted above were relevant in 1996, and they were, how much more relevant are they now? The spiritual life commission also released twelve calls to the international Salvation Army, all pertaining to the spiritual life. One specific call from the spiritual life commission was the call to the inner life:

The Call

We call Salvationists worldwide to enter the new millennium with a renewal of faithful, disciplined and persistent prayer; to study God's word consistently and to seek God's will earnestly; to deny self and to live a lifestyle of simplicity in a spirit of trust and thankfulness.

The Affirmation

We affirm that the consistent cultivation of the inner life is essential for our faith life and for our fighting fitness. The disciplines of the inner life include solitude, prayer and meditation, study, and self-denial. Practicing solitude, spending time alone with God, we discover the importance of silence, learn to listen to God, and discover our true selves. Praying, we engage in a unique dialogue that encompasses adoration and confession, petition and intercession. As we meditate we attend to God's transforming word. As we study we train our minds towards Christlikeness, allowing the word of God to shape our thinking. Practicing self-denial, we focus on God and grow in spiritual perception. We expose how our appetites can control us, and draw closer in experience, empathy and action to those who live with deprivation and scarcity.

Referenced in the call to the inner life are spiritual disciplines to be practiced by the believer. Spiritual disciplines are described as life patterns that direct us to God and disciple us more fully into the likeness of Jesus Christ.

In the journey of spiritual growth we are in partnership with the Lord—We can't do God's part. He won't do ours. Salvation Army Doctrines 9 and 10 illustrate this partnership effectively.

First, Doctrine 9 emphasizes the necessity of the ongoing engagement by the believer in our relationship with Jesus Christ: *We believe that continuance in a state of salvation depends upon continued obedient faith in Christ.*

Scripture is replete with language indicating the same—"Seek the Lord's face always" *(1 Chronicles 16:11)*. God's people are to actively humble themselves, pray, seek His face, turn from wicked ways *(2 Chronicles 7:14)*. God rewards those who earnestly seek him *(Hebrews 11:6)*. Jesus' words, "Seek first the kingdom of God" (*Matthew* 6:33) encourage us further. Finally, from Philippians:

> *Work hard to show the results of your salvation, obeying God with deep reverence and fear. For God is working in you, giving you the desire and the power to do what pleases him (Philippians 2:12-13, NLT).*

Come Roll Over Me   **133**

Clearly, when it comes to spiritual life and growth in godliness, we have a vital part to play. However, we recognize that Jesus is "the champion who initiates and perfects our faith" *(Hebrews 12:2 NLT)*. Thus, in the life of holiness, Doctrine 10 focuses on the Lord himself as the Sanctifier:

We believe it is the privilege of all believers to be wholly sanctified and that their whole spirit and soul and body may be preserved blameless at the coming of our Lord Jesus Christ.

The verse referenced in the doctrine is from *1 Thessalonians 5:23 (verse 24 included)*.

May God himself, the God of peace, sanctify you through and through. May your whole spirit, soul and body be kept blameless at the coming of our Lord Jesus Christ. The one who calls you is faithful, and he will do it.

In farming, to expect a harvest, the farmer plants the seeds and pulls the weeds. That's the farmer's responsibility in the growth, in the harvest. But only God can provide the soil, sun, rain and that mystery of life itself. Yet the farmer can't expect God to plant the seeds and pull the weeds. Similarly, in our spiritual growth, God has provided the redemptive work of Christ, given us the Holy Spirit, the Scriptures, and the Body of Christ. These we cannot provide. But He will not put that Scripture in our hearts, minds and mouths, force us to attend prayer meetings or Bible studies, or to do good deeds and live holy lives. Those are ours to do. Vigorously investing in our spiritual lives and the lives of others is, I believe, what the Apostle Paul meant when he admonished the Christians at Colossae and Ephesus, to "live lives worthy" of the Lord and of his calling *(Colossians 1:10; Ephesians 4:1)*.

In our approach to spiritual life and growth in godliness, let us remember—

We can't do God's part. He won't do ours.

It is entirely possible for us to be absurdly busy working for God and the Army, while also being spiritually lazy, not prioritizing rightly according to the economy of the Kingdom of God, not prioritizing first things first—seeking God's face, studying the Bible, gathering for prayer, sharing in deep fellowship with other believers. Imagine you saw a friend straining to push their car down the street because they were out of fuel. When offered the suggestion of stopping to refuel, your friend refused, continued their strenuous and ineffective labor of pushing their car on their own strength, stating they didn't have time to stop and refuel.

Similarly, in our haste and hurry, we can tell ourselves we don't have time to stop and spend in seeking the Lord, while laboring and straining, running on empty, in service to the Lord. This is not an effective long-term strategy for effective witness for Christ on planet earth.

Clearly, Kay and Paul have prioritized well. They have lived in the way of wisdom, as Jesus described in *Matthew 25*, of the wise virgins who kept their lamps full of oil, fresh with the Spirit, even in the waiting, even in the night, in times of darkness. This is affirmed by Christ and embodied in the Raders.

Following the example of Paul and Kay Rader, may the Lord give us grace at this time in history, to be people who are characterized with intense hunger for God and his righteousness, and who exercise forcefulness of spirit, in our struggle against sin, and our eagerness to do what is right.

From the days of John the Baptist until now, the kingdom of heaven has been forcefully advancing, and forceful people lay hold of it (Matthew 11:12 (NIV).

Blessed are those who hunger and thirst after righteousness for they shall be filled (Matthew 5:6).

Train yourself to be godly. For physical training is of some value, but godliness has value for all things, holding promise for both the present life and the life to come (1Timothy 4: 7b-8).

Living Echoes Of Thy Tone [1]

"I Want A Principle Within"

Lyell M. Rader Jr.

Holiness appears to be out of date, from an age that has long since passed and now seems alien to the discontinuous forms and syncopated rhythms of modern life. Paul Evdokimov [2]

We must and we will maintain our holiness standard in both our teaching and our experience... We owe it to our children and our children's children. They look to us for the teaching that will direct them into full salvation, and they will narrowly and constantly scan our lives to find in us an example of its fullness and beauty... Samuel Logan Brengle [3]

The patriarch Enoch was a shoemaker, according to a rabbinical story. "With every stitch by which he joined the lower leather of the shoe to the upper, he united the Glory that is below with the Glory that is above." [4] Every generation of Salvationists is set the task of hallowing the mundane with the glory of the eternal, of pointing and embodying the way of holiness for our place, our time. In *The Call to Perfection,* Samuel Chadwick wrote a generation ago: "Truth needs to be reborn. Words change their content, and lose their value... New problems call for new developments. Faith must speak in new tongues, if it would cast out devils and heal the diseases and wounds of the world." [5]

Lyell Rader, who soldiers at the Bethlehem, Pennsylvania Corps, continues to preach, teach, write and mentor as opportunities arise. At his home corps, he teaches an adult Sunday School class and has served faculty terms at a variety of higher educational institutions. Of Paul and Kay, he writes: "While engaged in global ministry, they have been remarkably attentive to the cultivation of family bonds. The distinctive strengths of their leadership have marked all Salvationists: their theological depth, their passion for mission, their accent on gender partnership, their promotion of critical dialogue and their pulpit art."

Jesus is our model. His characteristic mode of teaching was indirection. As Emily Dickinson put it, "Tell all the Truth but tell it slant/ Success in Circuit lies/ Too bright for our infirm Delight/ The Truth's superb surprise."[6] Jesus engaged the hearer through folksy stories, evocative metaphors, dramatic actions. He embodied the truth he taught. He set pictures deftly in the gallery of the mind. It is in these images that we find the enduring themes of his holiness teaching. There are four clusters.

Life Together

First, and pervasively, are images of the kingdom of God. Holiness, in Jesus' view, is a manner of life together. He adopted a fraught and familiar picture of a promised kingdom. In the popular mind, the kingdom would, by upheaval and violence, settle scores and elevate Israel to the privilege and dominance she deserved.

But Jesus imaged his upside down kingdom by a basin (John 13:1-15), a child (Luke 18:17), a banquet (Luke 14:16-24), and a cross (Mark 10:45). In the Father's house is room for all (Luke 16:19-31; 18:9-14; Matthew 21:28-31, etc.). Entrance is by gift (Luke 12:32) and birth "from above" (John 3:5). Its fullness lies ahead (Matthew 6:10; Luke 13:29) but the kingdom emerges even now (Luke 17:20).

Holiness in these images is entirely equable. It is the kingdom's native air. All who believe belong. All bear the Father's signature (Luke 12:32; Ephesians 1:1, etc.), no rank, no partiality. It is the peaceable kingdom.

Not *from* this world (John 18:36) yet the kingdom flowers here (John 17:18). As Dag Hammarskjold, Secretary General of the United Nations, wrote in his bedside diary, 1955, "In our era, the road to holiness necessarily passes through the world of action."[7]

Growth and Harvest

Perhaps the most endearing images came from our Lord's boyhood in the fields around Nazareth. He found pictures of holiness in living things. Here is the seed of the word that grows in good soil (Matthew 13:3-23; Mark 4:3-20; Luke 8:4-15). It has a dynamism within itself (Mark 4:26-29) beyond our prediction or control. Its beginnings seem trifling (Matthew 13:31-32, etc.). Weeds intrude (Matthew 13:24-30). But harvest is assured—beyond imagination (Matthew 13:8).

The most extended metaphor is that of vine and branches (John 15:1-17). The Father is the farmer who tends and prunes the vine. "If we only saw the whole," said Robert Murray McCheyne, "we should see that the Father is doing little else in the world but training his vines." [8] Fruitfulness depends upon union of branch and vine, the vital source. We have but to abide (John 15: 4, 5, 6), in a love connection (John 15:9, 10, 17), to grow in Christ-likeness in character, conduct and mission. The Father has chosen and placed us to bear his fruit. As he faced vast non-Christian audiences in India, E. Stanley Jones would always recite in silent prayer the text, "You did not choose me, but I chose you. And I appointed you to go and bear fruit, fruit that will last..." (John 15:16).

The seed, pointedly, is the word of the kingdom, implying a disturbing critique of the church's practice. Donald Burke, president of Booth University College, Winnipeg, warns: "... Although we affirm Scripture's importance, biblical literacy among Salvationists (and other Christians) is diminishing rapidly." [9] This is one reason Calvin Miller gives for the "fading" of the evangelical church in North America.[10]

The growth of the seed in us may be fitful and slow, but a subtle power not our own is in play. "His supernatural love and life more and more invading, growing up in us; His sap rising quietly and secretly in the soul, bringing forth, not merely nice devotional flowers—but fruits." [11] Such is the progressive nature of holiness. The prayer of George MacDonald is fitting:

Make me all patience and all diligence;
Patience, that thou mayst have thy time with me;
Diligence, that I waste not thy expense
In sending out to bring me home to thee.
What though thy work in me transcends my sense –

Too fine, too high, for me to understand –
I hope entirely. On, Lord, with thy labor grand.[12]

Water and Spirit

A third cluster reaches back to the archetypal image of cleansing, life-giving water. The forerunner John announces, "I have baptized you with water but [one who is coming] will baptize you with the Holy Spirit" (Mark 1:8). In the shallows of Jordan, John demurs, "I need to be baptized by you and do you come to me?" Jesus insists, "Do it. God's work, putting things right all these centuries, is coming together right now in this baptism" (Matthew 3:15, Message). Sister Vandana, writing from a pluralistic Indian context, comments: "Christ standing in the Jordan waters might be taken as a sign and fulfillment of all the washings, bathings, purifications— for the sins of all men, of all times." [13] It is here in baptism that the Spirit, pictured as a dove, inaugurates the ministry of Jesus (Matthew 3:16-17). "No one can enter the kingdom of God without being born of water and Spirit," Jesus tells baffled Nicodemus (John 3:5). And to a stranger of Samaria, parched of soul, he promises a Spirit like "a spring of water gushing up to eternal life" (John 4:13-14). Nor is the Spirit gift for just a few. "Out of the believer's heart," Jesus cries aloud above the festival din, "shall flow rivers of living water" (John 7:37-39).

The Passion approaches. In a second-story room in Jerusalem, Jesus introduces the Spirit as teacher, helper, witness and guide (John 14:16; 15:26; 16:7-12). Capping the astonishing drama of events, he says farewell with the promise, "See, I am sending upon you what my Father promised; so stay here in the city until you have been clothed with power from on high" (Luke 24:49; John 20:21-22).

The Spirit baptism at Pentecost marks the inauguration of the church and still defines entrance into the Christian fellowship. In keeping with our militant motif, Salvationists mark enlistment into the missionary company of Jesus by a swearing-in ceremony under the tri-color banner of Father, Son and Spirit. As the Report of the International Spiritual Life Commission says: "The Salvation Army rejoices in the truth that all who are in Christ are baptized into the one body by the Holy Spirit (I Corinthians 12:13)... [The swearing-in of a soldier] is a public response and witness to a life-changing encounter with Christ which has already taken place, as is the water baptism practiced by some other Christians."[14] The imagery persists among us. "O rise, Immanuel's tide/And my soul overflow."[15]

Call and Cross

The fourth cluster of images is found in Jesus' call to follow—first to Peter and Andrew, then James and John and Matthew (Mark 1:17,19; Matthew 9:9), and the full complement of disciples (Mark 3:13-19). The image is that of a rabbi and his novices. Ordinarily, it is the aspiring student who would seek the privilege of being the guru's disciple. But here the roles are reversed. "He...called to him those whom he wanted... He appointed twelve...to be with him and to be sent out to proclaim the message..." (Mark 3:13-14). It is a call to a lifetime of following and learning. It has the form of an invitation but the augustness of a command.

Later the summons extends to all: "He called the crowd (*ochlos*, the poor and marginal) with his disciples, and said to them, 'If any *want* to become my followers, let them deny themselves, and take up their cross and follow me.'" Bluntly, the conditions are named: deny self, take up the cross (Mark 8:34; Matthew 10:38; Luke 9:23; 14:27). These are dangerous, decisive actions.

The setting of self-denial in the text is the imperial courtroom, where Christians must opt to confess Christ, at the risk of their lives, or spurn him (Mark 13:9-13). To deny self is to say no to our toxic self-absorption, our personal idolatry. "It seems that God's Spirit has to take every forward-moving soul through a drastic process of self-exposure. That undiscovered self-principle lurking in the depths, that root of sin, has to be looked in the face...."[16] This is the point of critical encounter. "Salvationists believe," writes General Paul Rader, "that when the love of God evokes the surrender of the soul's inner citadel to the lordship of Christ, there is a crisis of inner cleansing, a radical reordering of the person's vital priorities in terms of his or her new identity in Christ. The result is a continuing hunger for God and His righteousness expressed in a disciplined pursuit of godliness and daily submission to his will." [17]

To take up the cross is to accept the vocation of overcoming evil with self-sacrificing love. Amy Carmichael, legendary missionary to India, wrote:

From prayer that asks that I may be
Sheltered from winds that beat on Thee,
From fearing when I should aspire,
From faltering when I should climb higher,
From silken self, O Captain, free
Thy soldier who would follow Thee. [18]

We give thanks that General Paul and Commissioner Kay Rader have, in global ministry, sounded these themes of Jesus in living echoes of His tone.

God So Loved The World

"Deep Ocean Of Love"

Shaw Clifton

W hen Paul Rader was active as the General of The Salvation Army he had a vision of numerical expansion and of a million Salvationists marching across the globe. At that time my wife and I were serving as the leaders of the Army in the Moslem land of Pakistan where we evangelized, not among Moslems for that was illegal, but among the ethnic minority who called themselves "Christian" but used that term merely as an ethnic label and offered no explicit allegiance to Christ. We were able to focus on this group and lead many of them into faith in Jesus as Savior.

General Rader gave tremendous encouragement as we reported numerical growth in the Army year after year. We took the words of Jesus recorded for us in John 3:16 and applied them to Pakistan: "God so loved the world—including the peoples of Pakistan—that He gave His one and only Son..."

It was Nicodemus who first heard these words spoken. He changed as a result, not right away but he moved from being a clandestine follower to stepping out openly when Jesus was crucified. He went to ask for the body of our Lord. He had heard and accepted the words of Jesus: "Whoever believes... not perish... have eternal life... to save the world... not condemned... comes into the light..." (John 3:16-21).

Shaw Clifton, who soldiers at the Bromley Temple Corps in South East London, first met the Raders in person when he was the divisional leader in Massachusetts, USA, during a USE Territorial Congress. He reflects, "Paul promoted me twice and moved me with Helen from London to Boston and then to Lahore, Pakistan. I admire Paul's intellect." Having now entered retirement, Clifton is now free to write, accept invitations, lead Bible studies and give lectures. Clifton is the proud father of three great offspring and grandfather to six lovely grandchildren. And, of course, he was also the 18th General of The Salvation Army.

Not everyone hears and believes. John's Gospel records the skepticism of Philip: "Lord, show us the Father and that will be enough for us" (14:8). He wanted some sort of proof. We cannot condemn him; he was simply being human. Philip speaks for many of us. How convenient it would be to have tangible proof of God. Then we could humiliate the unbelievers! But wait a moment—maybe God does not want them humiliated.

Think of 1 Timothy 6:16 where we read about God, his transcendence, his immortality: he alone is immortal; he lives in unapproachable light; no one has ever seen him or can see him. However, then link that with John 1:18: "No one has ever seen God; the only Son, who is in the bosom of the Father, he has made him known" (RSV). God is so superior to us, yes! But Jesus has shown us what he is like!

The New Testament Greek words help us to go deeper into John 1:18, an essential precursor for 3:16. "Seen" is from the Greek *horao*, which carries the sense of "being admitted into someone's presence." The "bosom" of the Father comes from *kolpos*, which was a fold in a garment worn across the chest, like a pocket. "Made known" is translated from *exegeomai* meaning "to lead out and make visible to all present."

So putting these various strands together we can render John 1:18 in this way: "No one has ever been admitted into the presence of God, except the only Son who is in the most intimate relationship possible with the Father, and He has led Him out so that He is visible to us all."

When Nicodemus had his encounter with Jesus, and when this sophisticated, refined Jewish leader heard Jesus speak, he was in fact conversing with "the only Son in the most intimate relationship possible with the Father." Colossians 1:15 goes even further and confirms for us that Jesus is the image of the invisible God, and then 2:9 states that in Jesus there lived, in a completely human and bodily way, the whole fullness of God. It is hard to take in, but Scripture is telling us that we can indeed see God, just as did Nicodemus. By looking at Jesus we can look at God. Jesus said to Philip: "Anyone who has seen Me has seen the Father" (John 14:9, NIV).

Turn your eyes upon Jesus,
Look full in His wonderful face,
And the things of earth will grow strangely dim
In the light of His glory and grace.

Paul and Kay Rader were called by God long ago to be carriers of this message to all parts of the globe. Leaving home they launched out into unknown paths that would take them to Korea, where they immersed themselves in another culture and another language year upon year. Helen and I were blessed to meet up with them there when we gathered to celebrate the centenary of the Army's birth in that land. Then after Korea and a return to the USA, where Paul became the General, they gave themselves unstintingly to the wider Army world—a world that God loves so much that He gave us Jesus to prove it to us.

General Rader shared William Booth's vision of ministering as an Army to the whole needs of a person. The Army's soul-saving work is not separate from its social outreach. These are two sides of the same coin. Body and soul are not distinct. Each is integral to the whole person. When Jesus met the paralyzed man (Mark 2:1-12), He ministered to the whole of his needs. This man longed desperately for movement in his limbs but first he needed a revolution of the heart. To those looking on, only a physical cure would be convincing, for they saw the illness as the result of sin. Jesus did not condone their belief but made allowance for it. He proved the effect of forgiveness by making the man able to walk.

Booth's Army, Rader's Army, is called to serve people in this same way. James 1:27 (NIV) speaks to us of the nature of "religion that God our Father accepts as pure and faultless." It is this: "to look after orphans and widows in their distress and to keep oneself from being polluted by the world." Then again in 2:17, "Faith by itself, if it is not accompanied by action, is dead."

So Booth would first get rid of a man's raging toothache before seeking to impress matters of faith upon him. That "toothache" can take many forms and hence the wide diversity of Salvation Army social outreach: food centers; hostels for women, men and children; prison visitation and aid schemes; work with alcohol and drug addicts; schools; hospitals; homes for those in later life; institutes for the blind; emergency response units; etc., etc. The list could go on and on. It is all for Christ, to honor Him, to represent Him, to work in His name.

However, even though Salvation Army social programs can clear up the symptoms of sin, they cannot ever get rid of the sin itself. There is no permanent hope for a person—any person, socially needy or otherwise—without a lasting change of heart. Only God is the Author of such a change. "You must be born again."

Paul Rader's call to the Army was to lead people into faith in Christ and for us never to settle for social help alone. We will never, ever force our faith upon a person, or even make someone feel uncomfortable by talk of religious commitment. However, the lenses through which we see the world, the world God loved so much and goes on loving unstintingly, are entirely spiritual. Each person is a soul for whom Jesus died. So we will fight for social justice, but we will battle also for spiritual victory in the heart of a person. We will recognize the immediate, practical need, but we will see deeper than that.

God so loved the Raders that He called them into paths of sacred service. I wonder, as I pen these words in tribute to the General, if there is a reader who is hearing that same, persistent, sacred call. We hear it with faculties beyond our five physical senses. We receive it deep within our spiritual senses until it almost deafens us and we can do no other than respond. God still loves the world. God still loves you. What will you do about that? How far from home are you ready to go because of that? "God so loved the world that he gave…" Now what will you give?

Covenant

"Take My Life and Let it Be"

James Read

In his 1995 foreword to my father's book *Keepers of the Covenant* (Read J. E., 1995), General Paul Rader wrote: "If you want to know what makes the [Salvation] Army tick at its best, then you must understand the compelling significance of Covenant... It is not a word in general parlance, admittedly. And the concept that underlies it may be even more alien to our age...[But] we never needed to understand it more than now."

The situation has not changed in the 20 years since General Rader penned those words. Covenant still needs to be understood, and covenant still needs to be lived.

From a Christian standpoint, we would say this is because covenant is central to a biblically formed worldview. As Gary Herion put it in the *Eerdmans Dictionary of the Bible*: "to study the biblical notion of 'covenant' is...to study what is arguably the central or core concept of the entire Bible" (Herion, 1987). Or as the *Anchor Bible Dictionary* says, "the attempts of biblical theologians to find a thematic "center" (Mitte) of the Bible invariably return time and time again to the subject of covenant, or to some particular aspect of covenant" (Freedman, 1992).

James Read, soldier of Heritage Park Temple in Winnipeg, Canada, serves on several SA bodies, including Booth University College, Ethics Center (as executive director), International Social Justice Commission (senior policy analyst), International Doctrine Council, and Bible Study leader at his corps. He first knew the Raders through his parents but met the General at a USA National Social Services conference and both Paul and Kay while they led the USA Western Territory. Their biggest influence on Read is the way in which they are committed in word and deed to a goal-directed, mission-guided, ethically-principled approach to ministry (seen first clearly in their Mission 2000 campaign in USA Western and the "Press On" (Philippians) motto.

God's covenant is understood to be primary. It is then taken to provide a motivation for the formation of covenant relationships between human beings and a criterion against which to assess the goodness of such covenants. That is, for instance, why my father structured *Keepers of the Covenant* in two parts—first "His [i.e., God's] Covenant"; then "Our Covenant"—and explained that "believers who commit themselves in covenantal terms, as many Salvationists do, are simply seeking to respond appropriately to God's amazing commitment of Himself. The covenant that admits us to soldiership is an instance of this. A wedding vow is another..."

But how are we to understand the notion of divine covenant that is at work here? As General Rader noted, covenant not a word used in everyday English, so we cannot just assume the "person-in-the-street" meaning and transfer it to sacred contexts. Nor, however, can we simply rely on a study of the Hebrew and Greek words of the Bible that have been translated "covenant." While the Greek *diathēkē* was a commonly used word in biblical times, it primarily denoted a person's last will and testament, and that is too restrictive for understanding God's covenant with people. And the Hebrew *běrit* had too wide a meaning in general usage, covering as it did *any* form of a promise taken under oath, submitting oneself to suffer serious penalties for failure to keep one's word. What really is needed is a discerning reading of the whole text of Scripture, using these ancient words as indicators, but also using one's ability to make sense of particular narratives and the whole narrative arc of Scripture, and relying on one's own experience with God as one reads.

Let me explain. If we relied only on the concept of *běrit,* we could read the story of God's covenant given at Sinai and mediated by Moses as the story of a treaty imposed unilaterally on a people who submit to obedience as God's vassals, acknowledging that God is mightier than Pharaoh and has taken them out of Pharaoh's control. That, after all, is the sort of *běrit* treaty "negotiated" by many overlords the ancient Hebrews would have known of. Whether the divine covenant was seen that way at first or not, it is a fair characterization of the way it came to be seen by the time of Israel's great prophets, Isaiah and Jeremiah. Isaiah wrote of "good Israelites" who made a public show of adherence to the law to satisfy or perhaps to curry favor with God, but chafed at the restrictions that had been imposed and/or objected to God's tardiness in distributing the benefits they expected as compensation for their compliance.

To which God hotly retorts, "Is this the fast I want?" (Isaiah 58:6) What God really wants of Israel, Jeremiah reveals, is "a law written on their hearts" (Jeremiah 31:33); which is to say, God wants a willing, a desire-driven, and not simply a dutifully obedient response.

And if we follow the narrative of Scripture to the coming of Jesus, we see that God wants to present himself to people non-threateningly, non-coercively. God is willing to become Incarnate and have human experiences himself in order to effect the kind of relationship He really wants (and I believe has wanted eternally) with people. The Gospel of John tells the story of Jesus with his closest disciples just before he was betrayed by one (or more) of them, and prefaces that story with the words, "[Jesus,] having loved his own who were in the world, he now showed them the full extent of his love" (John 13:1 NIV). My father put it this way in my preferred version of his most well known song: "The basin and the towel, And *God* upon his knees" (Read E., 1998).

It is a story of love, of one party wooing another, giving extravagantly, yearning for a reciprocated longing for union. Paul says the experience we know on the human plane, an experience as old as Genesis of two people becoming one in marriage, is an apt illustration of what drives God and draws people into the relationship God wants (Ephesians 5:32).

The danger of coming at it that way is that one might infer that the divine-human relationship is predicated on the attractiveness of the parties in each other's eyes, as is typically the case when men and women "fall in love." But the Bible is replete with the message that God often actually finds people unattractive—for good reason. It is not the unfailing beauty of humanity, but the unfailing determination that he will make us "holy" (Ephesians 5:26) and make us "shine like stars" (Philippians 2:15) that moves God toward us.

The covenant that God extends to humanity is grounded in *agape*, not *eros;* a love that is faithful and reliable, enduring, tenaciously attached to the good of the other, willing to be long-suffering if necessary, transformative (see 1 Corinthians 13).

The covenant of God with God's people is best characterized by marriage, so long as marriage is rightly understood. The Apostle Paul teaches us (Ephesians 5:21-33) that thinking about what brings a man and a woman together in marriage helps illuminate the relationship between Christ and the church, and pondering the relationship between Christ and the church helps transform marriage into what it should be.

Marriage is in trouble in the 21st century west. One reason is that we see too few relationships that model themselves on the divine covenant. There are those who expect marriage to be one long hot, ecstatic erotic date in which two become the one they long to be. At the other extreme there are those who view marriage as a contract that defines the rights and duties of finances, property and custody, ended only by death or when the courts say it is ended. To the second, Ephesians 5 says seek marriage that is like God's covenant, not a bare contract, but a sustained, determined desire for union. To the first, Ephesians 5 says seek marriage that finds its sustenance in a covenant as unshakeable as Christ's for the church.

Marriage may be unique in the way in which it is able to correlate with the divine covenant, but approaching other human relationships with it in mind could transform them too.

I think, for instance, of the relationship with the sick. If "health care" were grounded in knowledge of God's covenantal faithfulness, what a good thing it would be. And what a tragedy when it is not. Modern health science has become so sophisticated, and consequently, the practitioners so specialized that attention threatens to become disease- or disability-focused rather than focused on the person who bears the disease or disability. Furthermore, science has made us so successful in treating diseases and disabilities that even person-centered interventions threaten to take cure as their primary goal rather than care. In contrast, Stanley Hauerwas says, Christianly understood "the physician's [and nurse's, and other professional caregiver's] basic pledge is not to cure, but to care through being present to the one in pain;" and "to learn how to be present in that way we need examples…a God who, we believe, is always present to us, both in our sin and our faithfulness" (Hauerwas, 1994).

I think also of our work relationships. The modern concept of a contract is not an unchristian concept, but for many lines of work it is not enough. At the heart of a contract is the idea of a sincere and enforceable bilateral promise of an exchange of goods and/or services and/or money, motivated by the self-interest of the parties to the contract. This pretty well describes many workplaces, but it corrupts others. To realize the good they are capable of, many occupations need people who do not only "work for hireling wages" (to quote General Albert Orsborn's pertinent poem (Orsborn, 1987)). "Contracts are signed to be expediently discharged," writes William F. May. "Covenants have a gratuitous, growing edge to them that spring from ontological change and are directed to the upbuilding of relationships" (May, 1998). It is not that a contract is self-interested and a covenant altrustic; it is that a covenant is intended to be long lasting and focused on the relationship not just the parties to it. The promise of endurance makes possible a future together that cannot be seen or realized at the point of making the promise, and it is the spirit of trusting to unforeseeable future goodness that motivates the promise.

To draw on an example I know personally: at the point of seeking tenure, professors' research plans are not yet fully formed and so they do not know exactly what they are promising their universities. Professor and university trust each other enough, however, to commit to seek a future together, believing that students and the world will reap otherwise unachievable benefits. For similar reasons, although the well-known officer's covenant in The Salvation Army context is actually only between the officer and God, there are benefits for The Salvation Army and its officers to think of their relationship also as a covenant.

I personally think of my soldier's covenant that way. When God welcomes people into covenant, they become new people. In the language of the Bible, they take a new name. There is a real change in identity. So it could be with Salvation Army soldiers. That is, experientially, new soldiers and the believing community around them should see themselves as making a joint promise to be in long-term relationship with each other, resolving to venture into an unknowable future collectively, in the Christian hope that the result will not only redound to their own benefit but will literally transform them and flow over into good for the world at large.

Works Cited

Freedman, D. N. (Ed.) (1992). *Anchor Bible Dictionary* (Vol. 1) New York: Doubleday.

Hauerwas, S. (1994). Salvation and Health: Why Medicine Needs the Church. In W. G. Boulton, T. D. Kennedy, & A. Verhey, *From Christ to the World* (p. 387). Grand Rapids: Eerdmans.

Herion, G. A. (1987). Covenant. In A. C. Myers (Ed.), *Eerdmans Bible Dictionary* (Revised ed., p. 292). Grand Rapids, Michigan: Eerdmans.

May, W. F. (1998). Code and Covenant or Philanthropy and Contract? In S. Lammers, & A. Verhey, *On Moral Medicine* (2nd ed., p. 132). Grand Rapids, MI: Eerdmans.

Orsborn, A. (1987). All my work is for the Master. In *The Song Book of The Salvation Army* (p. Song 522). Verona, N.J.: The Salvation Army.

Read, E. (1998). *Jottings from my Journey.* Toronto: The Salvation Army Canada and Bermuda.

Read, J. E. (1995). *Keepers of the Covenant.* self-published.

Human Sexual Trafficking And The Ecology Of Holiness

"Rescue the Perishing"

Jonathan S. Raymond

Human slavery is thought to be a thing of the past, but it is one of the ugliest, deplorable, profane, worldwide realities of contemporary life. It is organized, big business, one of the most lucrative expressions of organized crime today impacting millions of victims directly. The United Nations formally defines human trafficking as follows:

> "Trafficking in persons" shall mean the recruitment, transportation, transfer, harboring or receipt of persons, by means of the threat or use of force or other forms of coercion, of abduction, of fraud, of deception, of the abuse of power or of a position of vulnerability or of the giving or receiving of payments or benefits to achieve the consent of a person having control over another person, for the purpose of exploitation. Exploitation shall include, at a minimum, the exploitation of the prostitution of others or other forms of sexual exploitation, forced labor or services, slavery or practices similar to slavery, servitude or the removal of organs.

Human trafficking is intense exploitation in forms of modern day slavery for the purpose of financial gain.

Jonathan Raymond soldiers at the Lexington Corps in Kentucky. He first encountered Captain Paul Rader when he was the guest speaker at the 1967 Asbury College Army Student Fellowship Retreat. Rader's key influence on Raymond has been exemplary leadership and sanctified preaching. Raymond, co-editor of Word & Deed: The Salvation Army's Journal of Theology and Ministry, speaks and teaches at SA spiritual retreats, leadership councils, and Bible conferences. He spent 39 years as a professor and administrator in higher education, including 14 years as president of Booth University College and Trinity Western University (both in Canada).

One of the most insidious forms of human trafficking exploits predominantly women and children, girls and boys, forcing them into the commercial sex industry—including prostitution, pornography, nude dancing, and being sold as "brides." A means of control over victims is forced addiction.

A voracious appetite for a supply of women's and children's bodies exists throughout the world. Traffickers simply profit by meeting the demand through recruitment, procurement, transport, and selling victims to meet the demand. The global marketplace is anywhere men purchase sex: brothels, strip clubs, escort services, bars, clubs, massage parlors, and pimp-facilitated, street-level prostitution.

Those who demand bodies to consume in commercial sex fuel the need for a supply of those bodies. Traffickers are simply supplying women and children through acts like recruiting, procuring, transporting, and the selling of persons to meet that demand.

From the Uttermost to the Uttermost

It may well be impossible for the average person to identify with and appreciate what victims of human sexual trafficking experience, the horror of their journey, their sense of abandonment, and their complete loss of self-respect and hope. Even when they are rescued from the clutches of their slavery, their years of enslavement, degradation, addiction and abuse remain with them. The toxic context of their plight leaves emotional scars and personal trauma for years to come. Memories need to be healed and positive self-regard and personal worth must be rediscovered. Once a victim is rescued from the scourge of modern slavery, where and how do healing and recovery take place? Under what conditions and in what context can she or he seek and find wholeness, peace, and joy? Is it even possible? The good news is that it is possible for victims of human sexual trafficking to experience transformation from the uttermost of the suffering and depravity of their past to the uttermost of health, healing and wholeness of their future.

Jesus said – "I have come that they might have life, and that they might have it more abundantly" (John 10:10). Speaking of the work

TSUNAMI OF THE SPIRIT

of the Holy Spirit, He said - "I will send you the Comforter ... He will guide you into all truth" (John 16:7&13). Jesus also said – "In me You may have peace. In the world you will have tribulation; but be of good cheer, I have overcome the world" (John 16:33).

Throughout Scripture, including the teachings of Jesus, we find the ecological metaphor. The ecological metaphor suggests that life does not exist in a vacuum, and that all organisms, including humans, live and die in environments (bio, social, and/or spiritual contexts). We live in all three ecologies (bio, social and spiritual) interacting with the nature of each environment. Victims of human sexual trafficking have experienced the uttermost toxic environments of exploitation and degradation where sin and suffering reign. However, this is not the only reality they may experience. The opposite biological, social, and spiritual context is possible, the ecology of health, wholeness, and holiness.

The Gospel message is straightforward. God created man and woman in His social and moral image for wholesome, interpersonal relationship with Him and each other—characterized by holy love after God's essence and likeness. In response to sin and the fall of mankind into sinfulness, God our Father sent Jesus Christ His Son to live, die, and be resurrected to make a way for our redemption, reconciliation, and restoration back to health, wholeness, and holiness. God's holy love was, is, and always will be directed to us through His grace. It calls for a response of faith and obedience to live and thrive in the context of his presence and continuing grace. By the continuing work of Jesus in us through the Holy Spirit, God uses us as human agency to provide love to others. He calls us to create the conditions, establish the environments, design and resource the ecologies of holy love within which God's grace brings healing and wholeness, restoration, and abundant life. This is the faithful response to God's plan for victims of human trafficking. The provision of services to rescued victims is helpful, but it is not enough to bring full restoration. In fleeing the toxic ecology of slavery, their recovery may be occasioned by healing contexts of God's holy love expressed by the human agency of others.

These healing social-spiritual contexts may understood as ecologies of holiness whereby in the dynamic engagement of victims with others of Christ-like support and compassion, they can find healing and wholeness toward restoration from the ravages of trafficking.

Ecologies of Holiness: Two Examples

Ecologies of holiness make possible a spiritual acquaintance process whereby persons become aware that there really is a God, that He really is present in their lives, and that we see God most clearly in the life and love, death and resurrection, and continuing work of God's Son, Jesus Christ, by the Holy Spirit. In such social-spiritual contexts, they come to faith in Christ and experience the presence and holy love of Christ through the compassion of others. In the supportive, caring Christian communities, God's agents of grace respond in obedience to God's calling for a ministry to victims of human sexual trafficking. Agents of grace are committed members of Biblically grounded faith communities who make room for victims and engage in the ministry of hospitality. Ecologies of holiness are "nutrient appropriate."

The immersion of a person into the social/spiritual context of God's presence and grace make possible exposures to the very things that help a person to grow in faith and experience health and healing. Such means of grace include God's Word, prayer, the witness of others, and practical acts of mercy and service (love) from others that address the most basic needs along the journey of recovery. It was the conviction of John Wesley that acts of mercy and service to others were the most prudent and efficacious means of many varied means of grace.

This paradigm of the ecology of holiness has been the long suit of The Salvation Army throughout its history. One example is the Army's addiction treatment programs in Honolulu, Hawaii for the past forty years, and one program in particular, Women's Way. In Women's Way, women diverted out of human trafficking into treatment can bring their children (who also have great needs). Over a period of nine months to a year they receive nutrition, health care, psychological and spiritual counseling and Bible Study. They experience the life of the earliest Christian community (Acts 2:42) and the means of grace (learning of Christ, fellowship, the breaking of bread, and prayer) that grew saints.

At the end of their stay they are given transitional housing and help with employment. The most significant part of their recovery is the brokering by staff of their spiritual life into Bible focused faith communities on Oahu, where they are loved, affirmed, and nurtured in their faith. The combination of Women's Way and these faith communities constitute "Ecologies of Holiness" where the love of Christ and the ongoing work of the Holy Spirit make possible more than mere rescue from slavery, but recovery and restoration to health, wholeness, and holiness. These are social and spiritual contexts that make it possible to heal and to grow in the grace of God.

Without such ecologies of holiness, victims rescued from human sexual trafficking and addiction remain vulnerable and are at risk of slipping back into the old toxic environments of their past existence. Inevitably there is recidivism and some victims do slip back. I am familiar with this particular example, because in 1980 it was my privilege to serve as the Chief Administrator of the Army's Addiction Treatment Facilities in Honolulu and establish the Women's Way program from its beginning.

Another example of ecologies of holiness with a potential impact on human trafficking is evangelical Christian colleges and universities. Not all, but many are powerful, effective contexts for growing godly Christian leaders of competence and character after the likeness of Jesus Christ. They go beyond merely the cognitive exercise of producing and conveying knowledge. They also develop students socially and spiritually from the point of coming to faith in Christ (justifying grace) to growing and maturing in God's grace, and encountering God in what Paul describes as being "filled to all the fullness of God" (Ephesians 3:19), holiness.

Such Christian college and university settings offer intentional exposures to a diversity of means of grace: Bible studies, worship, prayer gatherings, in-class discussions of faith matters, service opportunities to name only a few. They are intellectually, socially, and spiritually nutrient appropriate ecologies promoting the natural development of holy, godly graduates, many of whom graduate into fields and professions to establish ecologies of holiness in the various marketplaces of life. In the past several years, a passion for addressing the difficult, complicated issues of human sexual trafficking has emerged among students of Christian colleges and universities. They are the compassionate, human agency of the future through whom God may continue to address the global challenge of human sexual trafficking.

Compassionate ecologies of holiness are the ultimate answer to full recovery for victims of human sexual trafficking and for the recovery of all who are caught up in the sin of this worldwide enterprise. Such contexts of grace transform us all from the uttermost of degradation to the uttermost of perfect love.

Post Script: Recently I was invited to a fundraiser for PureHope, an NGO Christian organization devoted to responding to the blight of human sexual trafficking. My hosts were General Paul and Commissioner Kay Rader, who are on the board of directors of PureHope. While I am familiar with the work of the Army under their leadership, I more recently learned that their interest in addressing this tough issue goes well beyond the exemplary work of the Army. It is but one expression of their life-long passion for others and commitment to live lives of holy love. Thanks be to God!

Brengle's Teaching On "Shouting"

"Shout Aloud Salvation!"

Young Sung Kim

INTRODUCTION

Commissioner Samuel Logan Brengle's teaching on prayer is a rich subject for investigation, because prayer is located at the center of his holiness theology as well as his sanctified life ministry. Unfortunately, with the exception of David Rightmire's pioneering scholarly works on Brengle, [19] the many significant facets of Brengle's theological legacy have not been fully discussed in a proper theological reflection.

Having said that, I am convinced that the subject of "shouting," which is emphasized by Brengle as a distinct manifestation of extraordinary prayer, should be recognized as one of the most exciting and arguable themes in his holiness teaching. In this paper, therefore, I will examine Brengle's teaching on shouting in his writings, so it may bring a new perspective for deepening our understanding of Brengle's legacy of holiness teaching and his unalloyed passion for holy living.

Young Sung Kim, a soldier at the Spring Valley corps in New York, is the territorial ambassador for holiness in The Salvation Army USA Eastern Territory. He writes: "It is truly amazing when I reflect upon my life that has been touched and blessed by God's mysterious hands through General Paul and Commissioner Kay Rader ever since my youth from Korea. Particularly, in 1978, I was led to the altar and was assured of my calling to officership through the ministry of then Chief Secretary, Lt. Colonel Paul Rader, who delivered the Spirit-filled message at the territorial revival meeting. In 1996, I still vividly remember the thrilling yet overwhelming feeling that I had of the unexpected privilege to be commissioned and ordained as a Salvation Army officer by General Paul Rader. Furthermore, to receive words of blessing in my own native language of Korean at the Niagara Falls Congress was magical."

1. What is "Shouting"?

In *Helps to Holiness,* as a separated chapter,[20] we find Brengle's important teaching on shouting. In it, Brengle passionately urges us to know the importance and necessity of shouting, which is understood as a distinctive manifestation of extraordinary prayer. For Brengle, shouting basically signifies a vital spiritual sign not only for anyone who is honestly seeking God's blessing, but also particularly for the "Spirit-baptized" believer.[21] For Brengle, shouting is not an option for our spiritual lives. It is God's expectation for us to take into our ongoing spiritual battlefields. The importance of shouting in a sense of confrontation with ongoing spiritual warfare is stressed as follows. Brengle said: "nothing can stand before a man with a genuine shout in his soul. Earth and Hell flee before him, and all Heaven throngs about him to help him fight his battles."[22] "When there is victory, there is shouting, and where there is no shouting, faith and patience are either in retreat, or are engaged in conflict, the issue of which for the time being seems uncertain."[23]

Certainly, Brengle emphasized that shouting urgently needs to be demonstrated even in our ordinary worship setting. He pointed out that "many a prayer meeting has failed at the shouting point. Songs were sung, testimonies had been given, the Bible had been read and explained, sinners had been warned and entreated, prayers had been poured forth to God, but no one wrestled through to the point where he could and would intelligently praise God for victory, and, so far as could be seen, the battle was lost for want of a shout."[24]

2. Shouting and Waiting on God

For Brengle, essentially, shouting symbolizes a dynamic outward spiritual manifestation of the believer's inner desire for and assurance of being blessed by God's grace in the larger setting of waiting on God.[25] Brengle illustrated the context between the relation of shouting and waiting on God as follows:

...There are others who *wait* on God in secret places, who seek His face with their whole hearts, who groan in prayer with unutterable longing to know God in all His fullness and to see His kingdom come with power; who plead the promises, who search the word of God and meditate on it day and night, until they are full of the great though [sic] and truths of God, and faith is made perfect. Then the Holy Ghost comes pressing down on them with an eternal weight of glory that compels praise, and when they *shout* it takes effect. Every cartridge is loaded, and at times their *shouting* will be like the boom of a big gun, and will have the speed and power of a cannon-ball (Italics mine). [26]

To understand Brengle's emphasis of shouting in relation to waiting on God, we must observe carefully. As David Rightmire indicates, the importance of waiting on God in every aspect of Christian life is a continuing theme in Brengle's holiness writings. [27] Departed from the errors of Quietism (or "Stillness doctrine"), Brengle's position of waiting for God does not mean that we are giving up all human activity and remaining in passivity, including withdrawal of the means of grace in our daily Christian walk.

On the contrary, for Brengle, waiting on God is an ongoing persistent spiritual movement and activity based on the co-operant relation between God and human beings, which is named as the Wesleyan synergism. [28] Regarding the notion of the divine/human synergism of waiting on God (including shouting), Brengle pointed out that "we are workers together with God, and if we will praise Him, He will see to it that we have something for which to praise Him." [29] Despite the synergistic notion of waiting on God, however, Brengle also elucidated the fact that the essential condition of waiting on God is God's sufficiency only, and we must be waited upon. [30] He made clear this point as follows: "We must not forget that 'our sufficiency is of God'— that God is interested in this work and waits to be our Helper. We must not forget that with all our study and experience and knowledge and effort we shall fail, unless patiently, daily, hourly, we wait upon God in prayer and watchful faith for the help and inspiration of the Holy Spirit." [31]

3. Theological Interpretation of Shouting

Brengle's theological interpretation of shouting is worth examining in the larger spectrum of the Wesleyan way of salvation (*"via salutis"*), [32] especially focusing to understand the ways of appropriation of God's grace in the foundation of divine/human synergism. Brengle pointed out that:

> Shouting and praising God is to *salvation what flame is to fire.* You may have a very hot and useful fire without a blaze, but not till it bursts forth into flame does it become irresistible and sweep everything before it. So people may be very good and have a measure of salvation, but it is not until they become so full of the Holy Ghost that they are likely to burst forth in praises to their glorious God at any hour of the day or night, both in private and public, that their salvation becomes *irresistibly* catching (Italics mine). [33]

In this statement, Brengle indicates that the various aspects of the manifestation of shouting (along with "praising God") will show how God's salvific intervention can be appropriated into the people's hearts. Brengle asserts that there is a certain stage of shouting that leads us in our salvation to "what flame is to fire." Through the aid of the Holy Spirit, in this particular stage, our "salvation becomes *irresistibly* catching (Italics mine)." The crucial point is this: for Brengle, the genuine internal nature of shouting implies the salvific connection.

Considering Brengle's emphasis on the soteriological nature of shouting, I see that the result and possibility of the initial stage of shouting as described by Brengle can be viewed as the result and evidence of the work of God's prevenient grace (from the Latin *pre* meaning "before" and *venient* meaning "coming to") that bestows *irresistibly* upon this particular stage of human condition in shouting.

Allow me to elaborate further. I am fully aware that the traditional Wesleyan view of prevenient grace [34] is understood as *resistible* grace including other categories of God's redemptive grace: justifying and sanctifying grace which are also understood as *resistible* grace in the Wesleyan paradigm of the order of salvation (*"ordo salutis"*). However, in line with Kenneth J. Collins's theological argument,[35] I perceive prevenient grace as *irresistible* grace in regards to the logical follow up of Wesley's emphasis on original sin and human depravity.[36] It is understood that because of the total corruption of human nature after the fall, God's initial redeeming grace should be bestowed by God alone.

Following logically, *irresistible grace* has to operate at least at some point in the Wesleyan order of salvation.[37] In this point, prevenient grace (*as irresistible grace*) suggests that fallen humanity could not reject God's initial restoration of faculties. In regards to this theological perspective, although the setting is different, I suggest that there is interconnected theological implication between Brengle's way of description of the salvific notion of shouting and the context of how God's prevenient grace operates irresistibly in the process of God's initial restoration of the human faculties.

Certainly, Brengle continually stressed that shouting as a distinctive and vital spiritual activity must be applied and experienced throughout the whole process of the Christian journey, from the stage of "babies in Christ" (justification) toward the stage of "adult Christians" (entire sanctification) and until death (glorification). He emphasized that:

Shouting is the *final and highest expression of faith made perfect* in its various stages. When a sinner comes to God in hearty repentance and surrender, and, throwing himself fully on the mercy of God, looks to Jesus only for salvation, and by faith fully and fearlessly grasps the blessing of justification, the first expression of that faith will be one of confidence and praise. No doubt, there are many who claim justification who never praise God; but either they are deceived, or their faith is weak and mixed with doubt and fear. When it is perfect, praise will be spontaneous (Italics mine)." [38]

Here, Brengle stresses that every one of God's people must pursue the final stage of the spiritual manifestation of shouting, which is symbolized as "the final and highest expression of faith made perfect." In the light of the Wesleyan way of salvation, it is important to recognize that this stage signifies the result of the appropriation of God's blessing of entire sanctification subsequently following after justification. Brengle affirmed that this ultimate stage of shouting is bestowed by God who made us holy "through the precious Blood and the baptism of the Holy Ghost and of fire." [39]

Continually, Brengle emphasized that the definite way of assuring this blessing of "the final express of faith" will not be demonstrated in an ordinary form of prayer, "but praise and hallelujahs."[40] As Wesley affirmed, however, it is crucial to acknowledge that even in this stage of "the final and highest expression of faith," the sanctified are required to continually grow in grace in our *willful obedient* faith based on Christ's atoning sacrifice through the power of the Holy Spirit. In this way, then, our ongoing manifestation of shouting in faith will persistently energize the flame of sanctifying grace throughout our journey to holiness.

4. Shouting and Tongsung Kido

At this point, I want to briefly mention that the concept and strength of shouting in Brengle writings can be easily connected with the Korean Christian heritage of *tongsung kido*.[41] *Tongsung kido*, which literally means "praying together out loud," is a distinctive form of prayer that the Korean Christians have cultivated in their practice of faith. Like "shouting," *tongsung kido* is characterized as an extraordinary example of a fervent, persistent and earnest way of crying out to God. *Tongsung kido* is a significant and almost universal spiritual practice that has been a distinctive way of experiencing the Spirit filled prayer life among Korean Christians. As an important part of the prayer life of the Korean Churches, it is used both in public and private settings of prayer intentionally. Whether practiced in a setting of personal prayer or in public worship, *tongsung kido* is offered in a loud voice.

In particular, it is worthy to acknowledge that General (R) Paul A. Rader and Commissioner (R) Kay F. Rader must be fully able to identify the distinctive character and strength of *tongsung kido*

TSUNAMI OF THE SPIRIT

based on their own exceptional and influential missionary service in the Korea Territory of The Salvation Army from the period of the years of 1960s to 1980s.[42] The time they lived in Korea was one of the most crucial time periods in the modern history of Korea, not only in the socio-political aspects, but also in its religious aspect, especially from the experience of the Korean churches.

One particular religious phenomenon directly relates to the subject of the *tongsung kido*. In those two decades the Korean churches became immersed in a great revival movement as a new expression of the biblical Pentecostal experience. It is understood that at the bottom of this religious phenomena in that time period, *tongsung kido* was embodied and actualized as the Spirit-anointed medium for experiencing the immeasurable growth and spiritual awakening of the Korean churches, including The Salvation Army.

Conclusion

In *The Way of Holiness*, Brengle describes a paradoxical notion of "the secret of prayer." He said: "prayer is a puzzle to unbelievers, but a sweet privilege to us…That is the secret of prayer."[43] For Brengle, as we learned, *shouting* is an undeniable "sweet privilege" of believers. Our task is now to persistently taste it and live with it until we will reach the stage of "the final and highest expression of faith" in Christ who is the reason for us to shout!

Courage, Commitment, Compassion, And Competence

"Courage, Brother"

Bob Docter

Courage is a matter of the heart. *Coeur*, French for heart, speaks of one's spirit accompanied by self-confidence and vigor. The *Oxford Universal Dictionary* notes that by the seventeenth century, people thought of *courage* as "that quality of mind in facing danger without fear."

We would all like to be courageous, that is, until we face a situation threatening our physical self, our ambitious self, our status in relation to others. Then, our fortitude sways in relation to our ability to rationalize the cost/benefit of the action. The courageous person faces danger through triumph over fear.

Melanie Greenberg, Ph.D., writing in *Psychology Today*, notes that courage is a lot more than bravery. Like Martin Luther King and Nelson Mandela, others are willing to speak out against injustice and stand in the firing line to confront it and its evil brothers of racism, sexism, poverty or any form of the status quo that inhibits innovation and inclusion.

Greenberg has identified six attributes of courage with accompanying quotes from distinguished figures.

Bob Docter, who has soldiered at Pasadena, California, Tabernacle Corps for more than six decades (and four separate buildings), is Editor in Chief of New Frontier Publications, as well as band person and Sunday School Teacher. He worked closely with the Raders when they were stationed in USA Western Territory and finds in them a continual inspiration. Docter is former CSM (40 years), President, Board of Education, Los Angeles Unified School District, and a professor emeritus (still teaching) at California State University, Northridge (CSUN).

1. Feeling fear, yet choosing to act

"Can a man still be brave if he's afraid?" His father answered: "That is the only time a man can be brave." (A line from *The Game of Thrones*)

"Fear and courage are brothers." – a proverb

"Being terrified but still going ahead and doing what must be done—that's courage. The one who feels no fear is a fool, and the one who lets fear rule him is a coward." – Piers Anthony

2. Following your heart

"To dare is to lose one's footing momentarily. Not to dare is to lose oneself." (Soren Kirkegaard)

"And most important. Have the courage to follow your heart and intuition. They seem to already know what you truly want to become. Everything else is secondary." (Steve Jobs – Stanford commencement speech)

3. Persevering in the face of adversity

"It's not the size of the dog in the fight, it's the size of the fight in the dog." (Mark Twain)

"Courage doesn't always roar. Sometimes courage is the little voice at the end of the day that says: I'll try again tomorrow." (Mary Anne Radmacher)

4. Standing up for what is right

"Sometimes standing against evil is more important than defeating it. The greatest heroes stand because it is right to do so." (N.D. Wilson)

"From caring comes courage." (Leo Tzu)

5. Expanding your horizons: letting go of the familiar

"This world demands the qualities of youth; not a time of life but a state of mind, a temper of the will, a quality of the imagination, a predominance of courage over timidity, of the appetite for adventure over the life of ease." (Robert F. Kennedy)

"Life shrinks or expands in proportion to one's courage." (Anais Nin)

6. Facing suffering with dignity (and) faith

"A man of courage is also full of faith. (Marcus Tullius Cicero)
"The ideal man bears the accidents of life with dignity and grace, making the best of circumstances." (Aristotle)

Time after time, the Territorial Commander of The Salvation Army's U.S.A. West Territory from November 1989 to his election as General in July 1994, Paul Rader, along with his wife, Kay, continually demonstrated the qualities of great courage, commitment, compassion and competence.

This appointment was their second in the Western Territory. They were stationed at the Pasadena, California, corps for a few years during which Paul completed his doctorate at Fuller Seminary and Kay served in youth programs. She developed the Guard and Sunbeam program at the corps into the largest in the territory. It's always both—Paul *and* Kay Rader. I never think of them in any other way. They work together. They're a team, a combined duo, a perfect pair.

Then as territorial leaders, they served together attacking the responsibilities related to territorial leadership always with an eye for evangelism, soldier growth, personally and numerically.

The Raders arrived in the territory in November 1989 and went to work examining potential, assessing direction and getting to know local leadership. They didn't waste any time. In March of 1991, *New Frontier* trumpeted the large headlines:

Mission 2000 Announced and Plans Set To Double The Territory

New Frontier stated: "In a springtime promise of Easter renewal, Commissioner Paul A. Rader, Territorial Commander, has launched the West toward MISSION 2000, the most sweeping challenge of growth since the territory's early growth boom over a century ago."

"Is it time to hear again the Pentecostal call," Rader asked, "to see the vision and dream dreams as never before?" Rader asked that question while speaking to the territory though closed circuit video.

"If we respond in daring faith to the opportunities of this moment

in history, we must build with boldness toward the year 2000.
"This 20th century rushes toward the megamagnet of the year 2000. Demographers have already projected explosive increases for the western states. We are not beginning to keep pace with the population. We must move and accept the challenge."

In a box on the page, bold type defined the goals of a bold program.

MISSION 2000 is a bold, faith based venture to double the number of corps officers/leaders, and to secure at least double the number of soldiers and Sunday attendances by the year 2000.

Talk about chutzpah. Talk about courage. Talk about bold. Talk about expansion. He was committed to extensive plans designed to achieve significant growth. Then, he put the challenge to the territory. Commitment brought about the planning. He inspired the action, always giving credit to God.

Rader, along with several others, had worked for several months studying special demographic data from the 1990 census as well as a study by Church Information and Development Services. These data identified communities of significant size without Salvation Army presence. They also examined divisional corps planting objectives developed earlier by divisional teams.

Rader called the territory to action—to break free from the status quo. "What a time to be alive in Christ," he said.

Rader committed. It was full speed ahead to the millennium. He seemed to recognize that being fully committed to Mission 2000 preparations pertaining to a larger Army in the West made his job easier. It was freeing. While the major project did not limit the scope of his responsibilities, it did limit the scope of major emphasis. Commitment to a broad based plan allows an increased and more precise vision of a future to be achieved.

In order to facilitate administration and leadership he created two additional divisions in California—Sierra del Mar, with headquarters in San Diego and the Del Oro division with headquarters in Sacramento. They stimulated growth as they opened corps.

The territory moved along with an increased sense of urgency, facing the "Deadline Decade" of the new millennium.

On one occasion in the middle of all this planning, I went over to his office at Crestmont, deeply bothered by a matter over which he had no control. It was the situation in Rwanda when tribal fratricide raged and brought about the murder and rape of millions.

I asked him: "What's the Army doing about these massacres? Do we have a presence there? Do you think we would behave differently if the tribes were white?"

He answered, revealing his complete awareness of the nature of the tribal conflict still raging as we spoke, and was certain IHQ was addressing the issue along with the nature of our response.

We had other such "conferences." I discovered a depth in his belief system, in his very genuine faith, and in his commitment to the Army. I found an extremely well read, positive and creative person. Initially, I visited him searching for news and finally, I wandered over a few times simply to enjoy his company.

Sudden, unexpected events in the international Army caused some major changes in our peaceful planning process. General Bram Tillsley, elected to lead the Army internationally in April of 1993, relinquished his position for health reasons in May 1994.

Then, in late July, 1994, the High Council, representing territorial leaders from around the world, elected a new General of The Salvation Army. Several outstanding candidates accepted nominations, including Rader. With the votes tallied, the Council elected Commissioner Paul Rader, Territorial Commander of the Army's USA Western Territory. He was the first native born American elected to the office of General.

Because the office had been vacant, Rader became General immediately, and for one month filled both roles as the Army's international leader as well as territorial commander of the USA Western territory.

In late August, prior to his welcome and dedication in London, Rader took immediate steps to order the Army into specific and long term relief work in the bloodied and torn country of Rwanda, the heaviest populated country in Africa. Death figures due to murder, starvation and disease within the former Belgian colony approached millions. "This must be a long term program of significant proportion," Rader said.

A few days later, Rader was saying good-by to the West in a large meeting in Pasadena's Civic Auditorium. His presentation urged listeners to accept six specific commands drawn from scripture:

PRESS ON in pursuit of holiness and godliness; in response to God's call;

in response to the vision he entrusts to you and me; in commitment to a growing Army; in our commitment to stand in the path of pain to heal the hurting

FACE FORWARD – Sometimes reaching out means letting go! Be courageous

HOLD FAST – To our heritage; in the blending of our aggressive Gospel and social compassion; to our worldwide work; in our commitment to "the street"; in our appeal to youth

LOOK UP – We are people of God—look up; We serve the Lord Jesus Christ; We are citizens of a heavenly kingdom

STAND FIRM – Maintain commitment to the Lordship of Christ; the authority of the Word; the centrality of the Cross; in the possibility of grace for every human person; in the value of every human person; creative compassion; to our covenants with God, our soldiership and officership

REJOICE – in the experience of his *favor*; in the extent of *His Family;* in the evidence of his *Faithfulness;* in the embrace of this *Fellowship in the Gospel*

Whatever the challenges and opportunities before us, he urged us to PRESS ON!

In the early days of his tenure as General, Rader identified challenges facing the Army and set out to meet them.

"We are in a spiritual battle," he stated. "The challenges are spiritual without and within. We need to be a holy people, equipped and armored against the enemies of our souls."

• the challenge of spiritual inertia and self-absorption that works against commitment to the things that matter most
• The challenge to be who and what we claim to be: the Army of

God – militant, disciplined, mission-oriented, available, optimistic, loyal, compassionate, loving with the love of Christ, holy and Spirit-energized!

- Matching resources with desperate needs in a fresh understanding of internationalism as a joining of hands and hearts with Salvationists of every nation – a partnership in mission.
- Finding the right people – the best people for the biggest, most exciting, most rewarding, most meaningful job in the world – living out our faith in sacrificial service, compelled by love.

Speaking of the relationship of his previous role as territorial commander for the U.S.A. Western territory in relation to his new responsibility as international leader, Rader stated: "The West is a kaleidoscopic microcosm of the world-wide Army in its marvelous cultural diversity and spiritual dynamism."

Mrs. General Paul Rader (Kay) changed the perception of Salvationists concerning the role of a male General's wife. She recognized that the High Council elected Paul to be General, not her, and saw the use of the words "Mrs. General" as something less than powerful. I believe she reverted back to her rank of commissioner in order to accomplish important goals in the department where she had responsibility. Every General's wife since then has followed the same course.

Paul and Kay Rader—vibrant, vigorous and victorious Christian leaders.

The Run Up
(Salvationism and Mission)

"We certainly see the necessity of working toward the church being turned inside out..." — General Paul Rader, *Los Angeles Times* interview, September 3, 1994.

And now, hallelujah! the rest of my days
Shall gladly be spent in promoting His praise
Who opened His bosom to pour out this sea
Of boundless salvation, of boundless salvation,
Of boundless salvation for you and for me.

Hold On To Your Hats

"Tear Hell's Throne To Pieces And Win The World For Jesus"

Stephen Court

Our mission, our assigned task, can be summarized from a handful of biblical instructions buttressed by prophetic promises.

Instructions

"Go therefore and make disciples of all nations, baptizing them in the name of the Father and of the Son and of the Holy Spirit, teaching them to observe all that I have commanded you" (Matthew 28:19-20 ESV).

"Go into all the world and proclaim the Gospel to the whole creation" (Mark 16:15 ESV).

"But you will receive power when the Holy Spirit has come upon you, and you will be My witnesses in Jerusalem and in all Judea and Samaria, and to the end of the earth" (Acts 1:8 ESV).

Buttresses

"After this I looked, and behold, a great multitude that no one could number, from every nation, from all tribes and peoples and languages, standing before the throne and before the Lamb, clothed in white robes, with palm branches in their hands." (Revelation 7:9 ESV)

Stephen Court met General Rader at the mercy seat responding to Rader's compelling preaching in Vancouver. The Raders have been a model of visionary leadership for Court, who soldiers at the Crossroads Corps in Edmonton. Court, husband to an apostolic Salvationist and father of three warrior sons, is a prolific co-author who, on his good days, acts as a catalyst for mobilization.

""Behold, the days are coming," declares the LORD, "when the plowman shall over-take the reaper and the treader of grapes him who sows the seed." (Amos 9:13 ESV)

"The harvest is the end of the age" (Matthew 13:39).

Far from shamefully petering out at the end of history, the people of God, including The Salvation Army, which is the Fist of the Body of Christ, are meant to victoriously advance to "the ends of the earth," reaching "all nations," the "whole creation" with a disciple-driven, wonder-working, world-winning Gospel. And prophetic depictions indicate success is on the way, from the harvester overtaking the planter, of a harvest at the end of the age, of masses so large that no one can count, "from every nation, all tribes and people and languages" "clothed in white."

God means for us to win the world for Jesus.

Hold On

General Paul Rader and Commissioner Kay Rader warn us, *"Hold onto your hats. God is at work by His Spirit."* [1]

Now, during transposition, an inspired (?) typo inserted "e" into "hats," significantly changing the intent such that we are compelled to expose the new formulation. *Don't hold on to your hates.*

When you google the phrase "I hate what I" the most common conclusions to the sentence are as follows: ...I've become...I do...I look like. We might be dissuaded from God's kingdom purposes for us by these three most common hates.

i. *We hate what we've become.* In our most honest, self-reflective moments, we regret...

• our cooptation by the dominant culture, through which we are happy for a "seat at the table," funding, and goodwill at the expense of faith, sacrifice, and daring—we've become the tail, a big downfall from being the head;

- our accommodation with and in some instances embrace of relevance at the expense of the prophetic, beaten down over the years by 24 hours of hundreds of channels and hundreds of advertisements every day; we've become chameleons in search for a comfortable habitat;

- our compromise with the world, which allows us to vaguely represent the divine with an innocuous lower-case christianity following an ineffective lower-case god, as long as we avoid exclusive truth statements and assure that no one feels uncomfortable— we've become a neutered, spiritually impotent and innocuous organism.

ii. *We hate what we do.* We shake hands and kiss babies to promote our services, we hustle and bustle to land government contracts, we employ "song and dance" to entertain on Sundays. We do the work of lower-case christian performers and entrepreneurs.

iii. *We hate what we look like.* Whether our specific tribe and embarrassment over the outward attire or the whole family and its shameful moral resemblance to sinners, we abhor that we physically contrast and morally reflect "the world"—of it but not in it.

But, that is enough of typos.

The Raders exhort us to hold on to our HATS because God is on the move through His Holy Spirit.

You hold on to your hats when the unexpected happens, when things get out of control, when your world is turning upside down.

They are prophetic. Though on some fronts it may seem that things are slowing down, we can assure you that the big picture is different.

Jesus defeated Satan at Calvary and the empty tomb. So, victory is inevitable. It is a little simplistic to describe everything since that cataclysmic event as "mopping up" because there have indeed been setbacks and casualties. But, to save you flipping to the end of the Book (the Bible, not this one), we win.

Advances are being made all around the world:

- Scores of thousands of new people are submitting to the Lord Jesus Christ every day. [2]
- We're pummeling poverty at a global level. [3]
- We're thwarting the slave trade at the level of the chocolate bar. [4]
- Healings and other signs and wonders may or may not be more frequent than in the past but they are being reported more quickly and widely and so we hear of many wonders of the Lord. [5]
- People are getting sanctified and discipled. [6]
- Renewalist Christianity has been growing more than 4% annually for 40 years with no end in sight. [7]
- Evangelicals have quadrupled during the same time period. [8]

It really is an amazing time to be alive and fighting the great salvation war.

And it isn't just "over there" that this kind of thing is happening. The American chapter of the Assemblies of God has started 1597 churches in the last five years! For those keeping score that is 319 new churches every year in the USA.[9] And 1/3 of the denomination is under the age of 25! They've got a million youth in their American church.[10]

The thing is, God wants to go "super" on your "natural."[11] He wants to turn our world upside down. He wants none to perish—0— and all to come to repentance—7.1 billion. Jesus' reclamation operation that began 2,000 years ago is gearing up for the final battles.

It's completely out of (OUR) control! For those hunkering down to "us four and no more" and "rapture rescue" christianity, it is a complete shock! For the accommodating, coopted, compromising among us, it is absolutely unexpected.

Go Big

Raucous, stifled, feverish, celebratory. These and other colorful adjectives could only begin to depict the atmosphere at the farewell, reported in the February 21, 1880 edition of the *War Cry,* of daring pioneers headed from England, the birthplace of The Salvation Army, to its Acts 1:8 Judea on the other side of the Atlantic Ocean. Rachel Evans, Clara Price, Mary Ann Coleman, Elizabeth Pearson, Annie Shaw, Emma Eliza Florence Morris, Emma Westbrook, and George Scott Railton (we choose the order of naming them as the great Salvo egalitarians Kay and Paul Rader might) were gloriously farewelled to invade America at that meeting during which Founder Catherine Booth put the expedition in historic and eternal perspective:

> The decree has gone forth that the kingdoms of this world shall become the kingdoms of our Lord and of His Christ and that He shall reign, whose right it is, from the River to the ends of the earth. We shall win. It is only a question of time. I believe that this Movement shall inaugurate the final conquest of our Lord Jesus Christ.

It is in these words that the tiny sliver in the chart representing the combined people of God called The Salvation Army finds its destiny. While identity can't shape destiny, it can constrain it. Our hazy corporate memory has forgotten both...

- Our purpose—Saved to Save, as every pair of Ss on every uniform testify and,

- Our identity—The Salvation Army is a revolutionary movement of covenanted warriors exercising holy passion to win the world for Jesus.

Our negligence of our purpose and ignorance of our identity contrain us from fulfilling our destiny as prophesied by Catherine Booth. If we think we're an outmoded "Helping Group" [12] we won't be inaugurating anything. If we limit ourselves to being a church or an agency or an organization we're no longer the movement that God showed Catherine. If we think we are here to serve we are unlikely to be on the vanguard of the conquering forces of Jesus.

But, really? The Salvation Army inaugurating the final conquest of our Lord Jesus Christ?

You have to admit, it would be surprising, shocking, even. It'd be completely unexpected (well, except for a few of us). And it will be absolutely out of our control…

Still unconvinced?

"We do not begin to understand our capacity for advancing God's Kingdom purposes in a world gone wrong."— Paul and Kay Rader

Yes, the Raders are referring to The Salvation Army. How might we increase our understanding? What IS our capacity? Well, if we're settled that God's Kingdom purposes are to "turn the world upside down" as those long ago opponents worried, and if Catherine Booth was in the ballpark of accuracy of her prophecy, then this "Fist of the Body of Christ" role at the vanguard of the advance is the means.

World conquest? Impossible in and of ourselves. But we're not beginning to explore the endless treasure of resources, the limitless compassion our God has for a dying world, or the boundless salvation to which we have access.

Peter, in 2 Peter 1:3 explains,

His divine power has granted to us all things that pertain to life and godliness, through the knowledge of Him who called us to His own glory and excellence (ESV).

Paul confirms the Raders' concern about our capacity in Ephesians 3:20-21. You know it—watch for the "within us" bit:

Now to Him who is able to do far more abundantly than all that we ask or think, according to the power at work within us, to Him be glory in the church and in Christ Jesus throughout all generations, forever and ever. Amen.

Here's an alternative version:

Now this God, whose boundless force exceeds anything we crave or perceive, dynamically active within us, we, "the called out," magnify, in Christ Jesus, to every nation in this and every generation. Amen. [13]

The words attributed to evangelist D.L. Moody might not be entirely accurate, but they are challenging: "The world has yet to see what God can do with a man fully consecrated to him. By God's help, I aim to be that man." [14] God has found many who are fully consecrated to Him, the Raders included, and has used them to stamp the world with holy love.

So, let's submit to the process as suggested by Oswald Chambers:

The first thing God will do with us is to "force through the channels of a single heart" the interests of the whole world. The love of God, the very nature of God, is introduced into us, and the nature of Almighty God is focused in John 3:16, "God so loved the world ..." (1935, September 21). [15]

Then we will be positioned, downstream in the river of God's grace, to accomplish Samuel Logan Brengle's promise:

The whole earth is waiting for the unveiling, the revealing,"the manifestation of the sons of God," waiting for men and women, the boys and girls, who live in Christ and in whom Christ lives. When the world is filled with such men or controlled by them, then, and only then, will strikes and wars, and bitter rivalries and insane hatreds, and disgusting and hellish evils cease, and the promise and purpose of Christ's coming be fulfilled.

If you think the first couple of thousand years have been outrageous, just wait for the big round-up, the final chapter, the grand finale! What a wonder-working, world-winning ride it is going to be! Hold on to your hats!

Salvationism

"God's Soldier"

Harry Read

God wraps some of his gifts up in the oddest of parcels. A strange looking caterpillar becomes a beautiful butterfly; a pearl is created in an oyster shell; a magnificent flower comes from a dull, brown bulb buried in dull, brown earth while, out of the night, comes a spectacular dawn. Our heavenly Father takes the common ingredients of life and helps us believe in miracles.

Even so, who could possibly have thought that from a seemingly ordinary, evangelical open air meeting held outside an East London Public House in 1865, a Christian Mission would be formed which, in turn, would become a vibrant, international Christian movement? Perhaps an unusually perceptive person might have suspected that because the public house was named "The Blind Beggar" there could be an element of prophecy in the event and that God had a surprise in mind for the world; which, of course, he had. In truth, the degrading, drink-fueled behavior of the tavern's patrons merited the name; blind they were to God's plans for them, and beggars they were because their lifestyle impoverished them. Presumably, neither the publican nor his patrons knew our Lord has a good record with blind beggars, neither could they know this Gospel-meeting on their forecourt heralded hope for them.

Read, who soldiers at the Winton, Bournemouth, UK Corps, first met Paul when he was a delegate at the ICO, having set up an interview for him with BBC Overseas Service. In his words, "My wife and I were delighted when the High Council elected Paul as General. He looked liked a General and thought like a General, having the qualities of heart and mind to focus on relevant issues strategically, positively and encouragingly. He had the vision of a world leader who was the custodian of a rich spiritual heritage, which he was charged to pass on as a living, developing heritage to the next generation of leaders. In this important regard he obviously respected other leaders and the skills required to bind them together as an effective team. Read invests in intercession and a postal ministry that has grown in years subsequent to IHQ's No Heart More Tender, the book he wrote following his bereavement. A former long-time author of Words of Life, he continues to write.

Another event that might be regarded as prophetic took place 13 years later in 1878 when, discussing a proposed definition of The Christian Mission as "A volunteer Army," William Booth crossed out the word "volunteer" and inserted "Salvation." It was an act that seemed to open the floodgates of heaven. From that time onward this movement would be known as The Salvation Army.

In those destiny-laden moments, the moderately successful Christian Mission gave way to an Army, which, in a short span of years, marched its way through the cities, towns, and villages of Britain. They took to the streets and marched because the people were there. They marched because they were an Army with a growing awareness of their role as the vanguard of a soul-saving movement and, as they marched, they claimed the streets for Jesus. In faith, they claimed the best and worst of the people living there; the people whom society instinctively shunned, dismissing them as the "submerged tenth" of the city's population. But not so regarded by Booth's battalions of one-time "Blind Beggars" who were fighting on their home ground and knew both the language of sin and the language of liberty. With abandon they shared their new-found hope and love in Christ, telling family, friends and anyone who would listen, that though, *"the wages of sin is death, the gift of God is eternal life in Christ Jesus our Lord"* (Romans 6:23).

Our quasi-military rank system rather than conventional clerical terms should not mislead anyone; we are all the foot soldiers of Christ, the soldier-servants of the King. Our authority in leadership is subordinate to the aims of our movement and stems from Christ who came as a servant into our world and who calls us to serve him and humanity unconditionally. Our banners, uniforms, words and actions affirm our availability to fulfill the servant role. As part of Christ's body on earth we are privileged to do his work and do so with a contagious joy. That's Salvationism: that's the kind of Army we are.

Among the neglected, impoverished people of the overcrowded slums, conditions were right for a revival of the Christian faith. The hopeless found hope, aspirations were quickened, songs and testimonies of freedom challenged their despair, and joy, the joy of sins forgiven, the joy of a redeemed community, the joy of the Lord Himself, drew people like a magnet.

Rather than diluting the Gospel to make it more palatable to their disadvantaged hearers, William, Catherine and their associates presented a full message. They waged their war of deliverance with love and faith in a Christ who could redeem anyone and make anyone holy. The dynamic essence of their Gospel was: "from the uttermost – the farthest reaches of sin – to the uttermost – the most glorious reaches of holiness." No sin was more powerful than Jesus of Calvary. No heart, albeit soiled repeatedly by sin, was beyond the Holy Spirit's powers to cleanse, no prodigal was excluded from the heavenly Father's welcoming embrace, and the people responded in such numbers that the glory of God illuminated the dark corners of London's East End.

Salvationism was therefore, launched, tested and proved in the hardest of hard locations. Penitents knelt at mercy seats in halls and, in open-air meetings, they knelt at the strategically placed drum. Sins were forgiven and forsaken, homes were transformed and purest love blossomed as the new converts, embracing the Gospel, became saints.

How much they seemed to love this new Army with its improvised uniforms, unconventional music, informal leadership, adventurous spirit and focus on their needs! Inevitably, this innovative Spirit-led Army gained further acceptance and momentum. The momentum gained was breathtakingly unrestrained. In quick time the Army "marched" into other countries with such dramatic success that William Booth was able to convene an International Congress in London in 1886.

Since then many other nations have welcomed the Army with its practical Salvationism into their cultures, and the Army has lovingly and zealously nurtured its internationalism. Resources have been given where needed, and cross-cultural appointments at all levels have resulted in a bonding that is a source of satisfaction and strength. Different cultures have produced different styles of worship but the strategy is the same. We march under the same banner, share the same emphases and doctrines and obey the same Lord. And, wherever we are, we are recognized as an Army. Indisputably, internationalism is part of our Salvationism.

Our Salvationism owes everything to the Lord Christ. Because he died for the world and commissioned his followers to make disciples of all nations, we are embarked on a worldwide mission. Because we believe the Holy Spirit's guidance led to our distinctive name, with confidence we take in the front line of evangelism. The spiritually blind and those impoverished by sin need us, as do those who, for whatever reason, are down-trodden and economically poor, and do not those who are lonely, despairing, addicted, unable to cope need us? Young people, with life before them need us, as do all age groups. Our mission-field must include prisons, hospitals, nursing homes, market places, street corners and wherever people are being trafficked. Must we not also be where tragedy strikes? As a divinely created Army and as part of God's answer to human sinfulness we have no alternative; we have to serve.

In today's world, with its opportunities of communication, our role requires that we explore and exploit the mysteries and realities of cyberspace. We cannot leave this ever-expanding field to commerce and other interest groups: we must be there. And there—we are! Salvationism is not limited to yesterday's methods although many of those methods are valid and fruitful. Our faith and vision confirm that the less formal but potentially even greater opportunities of cyberspace are among the fields, *"ripe for harvest."* (John 4:35)

To sum up: our Salvationism means that, in essence, we are a "Blind Beggar" people, however we interpret that term. There are no limits to the aspirations of Christ-centered people. Born-again men and women, tutored by experience in the less privileged areas of our cities and gifted by the Holy Spirit, have become valued leaders in our local situations. Some have become officers proving themselves great leaders in national and international appointments. They have taken their places alongside others, also born-again, but from more congenial backgrounds who have provided leadership of the highest order.

Captains Paul and Kay Rader were following an honored tradition when, as an act of obedience to the Lord, they travelled to South Korea to serve alongside the Korean Salvationists. In the same tradition they mastered the language, accepting totally the new culture, its vision and opportunities. As they spiritually enriched their new fellow-soldiers, they were themselves enriched. It was a precious time in their lives.

Twenty-two years later they were appointed to their homeland and, in 1994, the High Council elected Commissioner Paul as the Army's fifteenth General. It was a huge task and a fitting honor as, jointly he and Commissioner Kay inspired the world-wide Army to live up to its heritage. They were committed to ensuring that The Salvation Army never lost its love for the blind beggars of this world or its calling to be the Army of the Lord. That they succeeded wonderfully well in their God-given task is now part of our history and we thank God for them.

We are an Army, mobilized by God
The cry of need our trumpet call;
We are an Army, pledged to fight for God
Until his foes before him fall.
Marching on with faith prevailing,
Marching on with hope unfailing,
Marching on with love travailing,
We are an Army, we are an Army
Mobilized by God.

The chorus is taken from the following song.
We Are An Army
High aloft earth's banners fly
In defiance of our Lord.
Christless souls his love defy
Rampant evil takes the sword;
'Gainst the host who flout his law
God, in mercy, goes to war.

Chorus
We are an Army, mobilized by God
The cry of need our trumpet call;
We are an Army, pledged to fight for God
Until his foes before him fall.
Marching on with faith prevailing,
Marching on with hope unfailing,
Marching on with love travailing,
We are an Army, we are an Army
Mobilized by God.
'Neath an empty Cross we fight,
Love's great sacrificial sign;
Emblem of his risen might,
Token of his grace divine.
Through this Cross, raised up for sin,
We shall conquer, we shall win.
Christ is with us in the field,
Leaves us not to stand alone;
Evil hands the sword must yield,
Christ will make the world his own.
Loud our songs of triumph ring,
Christ is Savior, Christ is King.

Words Harry Read
Music Robert Redhead
Written for Cadets' Commissioning Pageant, 1971
Published: The Musical Salvationist, July 1971

Evangelism

"Make Me A Blazing Fire"

Damon Rader

EVANGELISM STARTS AT HOME

My siblings and I will ever be grateful that our evangelist father and mother made our salvation and growth in grace a top priority. As a result, we all decided to follow Jesus at a young age. Before we were teenagers Paul and I started witnessing at the corps in open air meetings, on the corps Gospel Team and at school. Paul's sharp mind, good humor, creativity, and determination were evident early on. Later when we were roommates at Asbury College, I saw his passion and commitment to ministry in full force. He told me God had called him to "build a fire in people's bones," and he went on to do it.

He was diligent in developing his gifts and knowledge, earning three degrees before entering officer training. His Army service, with his wife Kay, in the States, Korea, and the world, is well known. Paul's gifts and anointing for multi-dimensional Gospel ministry both public and private, have blessed the Army world and beyond.

Damon Rader reflects: "There are many things about Paul that impress me deeply: his life, personality and character; the clarity of his purpose, and diligence in fulfilling his calling; the thoroughness of his preparation, and his life-long learning; the scope of his relationships within the broader evangelical community; his love and zeal for the Lord, and the power of his preaching; and perhaps most of all, his thoughtful, biblical approach to cross-cultural mission, and his mastery of Korean language and culture." This Rader, the founder of Salvation Radio in Zambia, describes his current war fighting: "My primary role is shepherding and intercession. I share oversight of the shepherding program of the corps, and seek to be responsive to the Spirit's promptings to pray for and with people in the corps and community. To the latter end, I am working at getting to know my neighbors."

He is a visionary, an innovative, inspirational leader, and his widespread ministry continues in retirement, here and overseas.

Evangelism is from the inside out, like God's other work in our lives. I believe it was Billy Graham who once said that:

"Evangelism is the Natural Overflow of a Spirit-filled life."
Natural to the nature of the source, who is the Spirit
Natural to the new self, created to be like God in true righteousness and holiness (Eph. 4:24)
Natural to the way God made us individually; not forced or faked.

Spirit-filled: inhabited, inspired, motivated, led, and empowered by the Holy Spirit.

Our inner being "wholly filled and flooded with God Himself" (Eph. 3:19 Ampl);

Filled with Jesus' own love, joy, and peace as we trust Him, overflowing with hope (Rom.15:13)

Streams of living water: Spirit-life that is full, fresh, free, and flowing <u>out</u> from our inner being – a gushing fountain (Jn.7:38), for the salvation of others.

Such a "wellspring of life" must be guarded diligently. (Prov. 4:25), (Cf. Phil. 4:7)

There is a **flow** to our faith-life that corresponds to the ways we love God with all our being.

Faith>Love>Obedience>Work/Witness>>
These are all active, consistent, and continuous.

Faith	Mind	Trusting Jesus as Savior, Lord, and God (Jn.20:28)
Love	Heart	Whole-hearted love, without Rival or Reservation
Obedience	Soul	"Not my will, but Thine be done" (Lk. 22:42)
Work/Witness	Strength	Strengthened in "every good deed and word" (2Th. 2:17)

Evangelism is a Divine–Human Joint-Operation – God does His part, and we do ours.

We can't do God's part, and He won't do ours, but He will help us do our part.

The Holy Spirit inspired the Scriptures, but holy men of God had to write them.

God will help us to know what to say and use our witness, but we have to speak.

God initiates prayer, and prays through us as we pray.

God expresses His compassion, kindness, and mercy through us as we act.

Evangelism is primarily a work of the Spirit

The Spirit is the One who illuminates hearts, Interprets the Word, Reveals Christ, Convicts of sin, Leads to repentance, Stimulates faith, Regenerates souls, and Transforms lives.

We are totally dependent on Him.

Evangelism also requires our Participation, and He depends on us.

We participate in the Divine Nature as Jesus lives His life in us. (2 Pet.1:4)

We participate in the Divine Revelation as lights in the world, in His likeness. (Phil. 2:15)

We participate in the Divine Mission as God works in us to will and to act … (Phil.2:13)

Evangelism is powerless without Prayer

Prayer is the chief way of cooperating with God, and without prayer there is no power.

Prayer is essential to the Spirit's work, before during and after conversion.

Prayer is an expression of our trust in God and our dependence on Him.

Fulfilling the Great Commission depends on fulfilling the Great Commandments

Jesus Himself put the two great love commandments together. If we love God supremely, we will love others, and want them to experience the extravagant love of God for themselves. But often people need to experience God's love from us before they can believe it, and accept it for themselves. Love opens human hearts, and then minds. How can we claim to love God and others if we do not care enough to seek the lost, pray for them, and share the glorious Gospel with them?

Evangelism requires two Love-Prayer Connections

Connection to God: in Loving Communion and Intercession - Walking with God
Jesus often withdrew to lonely places to pray and renew his strength. (Lk. 5:16)

Connection to people: Prayerful Love that cares, serves, listens and speaks — *Working with God Jesus* was constantly in the midst of needy people. He was a friend of sinners. (Mt. 11:19)

There is a natural and *necessary Rhythm,* that we see in Jesus, between the time spent alone with God in prayer and worship, and the time spent working with God among the people.
We must follow His example.

We are the *Medium* that God has chosen to carry the Gospel message; a medium that exhibits a message of its own that either reinforces or contradicts the Gospel.
We plead with people to be reconciled to God on behalf of Jesus (2 Cor. 5:20).

The power of the Word and the Spirit flows through us, but it can be distorted, degraded, or dissipated in the process if our lives are not clean, sanctified, and useful to God. (2 Tim. 2:21)

Evangelism is the responsibility of every disciple, and we are all equipped to participate.

There are many God-honored ways and means of bringing people to Jesus.

All means are needed, from mass to individual, remote to direct, and impersonal to relational. We may not be gifted and trained to preach to the masses, or to confront strangers with the Gospel, but there are ordinary, relational means that open possibilities for all of us.

There are various *stages of the Journey* from unbelief to faith, to wholeness, and fullness.
We have to really see and hear people in order to know them, to love them, and to win them.
God is at work in people's lives long before they decide to follow Jesus.

Their journey could begin with our loving interest in them, kindness, help, hospitality, and friendship, opening their hearts, and then their minds to hear and understand the Gospel.
That word could reach them through media, literature, Bible studies, personal sharing, etc.
When the Spirit convicts them and leads them to repentance and faith in Jesus, some may only need gentle guidance and prayer support, while others may need stronger encouragement, but not to the point of coercion. Jesus did not pressure people to follow Him.
Receiving Jesus must always be a free, whole-person decision.

After the new birth, immediate follow-up is essential, followed by discipleship unto holiness, incorporation into the church, and mission engagement.

We may not be able to lead someone through the entire process, but God has equipped us to contribute in some way, to some part of their journey.

God loves variety, and we are all different, but He is a master at matching us to the right people and opportunity.

Let's pay attention to what He is doing.

We may be gregarious, contemplative, pragmatic, intuitive, organized, or spontaneous.

We may have creative, relational, serving, or speaking gifts.

God can use what He has given us to bring people to Himself, if we keep it on the altar, and cooperate with Him.

In what *manner* should we speak? Perhaps I'm showing my age, but I don't like hype, high pressure sales, exaggerated claims, shouting commercials, and the like.

A winsome, gracious witness with humility, courtesy and respect is what appeals to me.

I like communication that is natural, direct, personal, and relational, that *listens* first.

It's foolish to speak before we listen. (Prov. 18:13)

Let's allow the Spirit to free us from all that hinders our witness, and keeps us from speaking:

Impediments such as secret sin that deadens conscience, disrupts prayer, and dissipates power; *Inhibitors* like fear, timidity, embarrassment, political correctness;

Inertia: no movement, no connection, no power; content to live vicariously, by proxy; asleep.

It's shameful to sleep in harvest. (Prov. 10:5)

God inspires and energizes us as we engage lost and hurting humanity.

Let's be **always ready** to give a reason for the hope we have in Jesus (1Pet. 3:15);

Daily prayed up, blessed full, fully *open* to God and the people — available and attentive; Anticipating in prayer who we might meet during the day, and what we might say (having relevant Scripture in mind), so we can seize every opportunity that comes, without hesitation.

It is an incredible privilege and joy to be part of God's redemptive activity in the world.

God has poured out His love into our hearts by the Holy Spirit. (Rom. 5:5)

May our hearts overflow by the Spirit in life-giving ways to others, whom Jesus longs to save.

Biblical Equality

"The Lord God Made Them All"

JoAnn Shade

As followers of Jesus, we live in a world that historically has not been a place of equality for all. Post-Eden, Cain and Abel introduced the pattern of sibling rivalry and one-upmanship. Those in power captured other men and women to serve as their slaves. Relationships between the sexes placed women in subordinate positions to men because of their gender, and ethnic and racial groups wrestled each other for power and control. Even modern-day groups of people who live under a sign of equality, such as the republic of the United States, discover that equality for all is a dream, not a reality. In declaring the independence of the thirteen American colonies, Thomas Jefferson may have believed that "we hold these truths to be self evident, that all men are created equal," but history tells a different truth, for "all men" did not include people of color, people without land or money, or people of the female gender.

In a similar way, the world Jesus was born into was not a world of equality. Slavery was prevalent, women were subservient to men, and religious and ethnic groupings each had their own hierarchies that kept the people of that day "in their place." So did Jesus change that equation?

JoAnn Shade soldiers at the Wooster, Ohio Corps, where she ministers in the shelter and social service programming. She first met the Raders when they were appointed as her divisional leaders in the PENDEL division in USA East. She and her husband were their corps officers as they soldiered at the Philadelphia Roxborough Corps. The Raders' biggest influence on Shade is the modeling of egalitarian leadership within their marriage. In particular, Shade notes, "Commissioner Kay Rader has breathed courage into me at critical times in my life." Shade currently enjoys a two-fold role: writing in a variety of ways both to explore biblical passages (current project is the teen women of the Bible), and bringing a biblical worldview to contemporary culture.

According to the proponents of biblical equality, yes, Jesus did change that worldview. One such group, Christians for Biblical Equality (CBE), articulates it this way: "The Bible, properly interpreted, teaches the fundamental equality of men and women of all ethnic groups, all economic classes, and all age groups, based on the teachings of Scriptures such as Galatians 3:28."[16] While equality in regards to ethnicity, economic class and age remain of vital concern to proponents of biblical equality, gender continues to be a main focus for the church at large and for The Salvation Army around the world, as it was the first biblically-defined difference between people, and continues to be an area of tension for many.

CBE's statement entitled *Men, Women and Biblical Equality* affirms that men and women are equally created in God's image; equally responsible for sin; equally redeemed by Christ, equally gifted by God's Spirit for service; and equally held responsible for using their God-given gifts.[17] Mimi Haddad, the president of CBE, explains Jesus' position: "Jesus assumed women were fully human and equal to men. And what is even more striking, he was also completely comfortable with women. He approached them as He did men, in public, regardless of cultural taboos. He offered them God's unconditional love, healing, and forgiveness. And he commissioned them to build God's kingdom (John 20:17-18), just as he commissioned men."[18]

New Testament scholar Gordon Fee encourages Christians to think bigger: "Perhaps the worst thing the evangelical tradition has done on gender matters is to isolate them from the bigger picture of biblical theology. Indeed, I think we are destined for continual trouble if we do not start where Paul does: not with isolated statements addressed to contingent situations, but with Paul's theology of the *new creation*, the coming of God's eschatological rule inaugurated by Christ — especially through his death and resurrection — and the gift of the Spirit.[19]

From its inception, The Salvation Army established a foundational commitment to gender equality. Christine Parkins explains that while "Catherine Booth accepted that the Fall had put women into subjection as a consequence of sin and that submission to the male was God's judgment upon her disobedience," Booth argued that "to leave it there is to reject the good news of the Gospel." [20] Booth's husband William was in agreement: "I insist on the equality of women with men. Every officer and soldier should insist upon the truth that woman is as important, as valuable, as capable and as necessary to the progress and happiness of the world as a man." [21] While he may have had a theological acceptance of gender equality, Booth's position was also a pragmatic one, as soldiers of both genders were needed for the salvation war.

Yet the Booths' vision struggled in its intersection with culture, especially outside the ranks of the Booth family. In her historical review of the urban religion of The Salvation Army in the United States, Diane Winston suggested that, "as the first Christian group in modern times to treat women as men's equals, the Army offered a compelling, if sometimes contradictory, vision of gender," [22] while Andrew Eason's work reached a similar conclusion: "If the history of the early Salvation Army teaches us anything, it is the fact that recommendations and principles, however well-intentioned, are not enough to ensure equality between the sexes. Although Salvationists made numerous pronouncements on the subject of sexual equality between 1870 and 1930, they failed to address the deep-seated assumptions and the discriminatory practices that worked against the possibility of an egalitarian environment." [23]

In an attempt to address these apparent tensions between foundational principles and organizational practices, international leaders General Paul Rader and Commissioner Kay Fuller Rader took on the challenge of broadening the role of women in ministry. What the Raders encountered was an uneven treatment of women most often affected by marital status, and described by biographer Carroll Hunt:

The Salvation Army legacy as told in literature and history reveals a divided heart when it comes to its women officers, trained and commissioned equally with the men, and at times handed what the Christian world considers "a man's job" but at other times ordered to stand back and stir the soup, preferably quietly. But the world contains an Army of women warriors called by God to service, and they are not about to disappear by drowning or discrimination. [24]

Commissioner Kay Rader articulated their position clearly and decisively: "From its earliest days, the Army's position of women in ministry has been clean and unequivocal. The Salvation Army finds no place for gender discrimination within its beliefs and practices. Whatever biases male-dominated cultures dictate, the Army's commitment is the empowerment of both women and men in ways consistent with the teachings and example of Christ." [25] In doing so, she worked to "help women realize their potential for ministry ... to be someone to stand in the gap for them in any way I could, to keep Catherine Booth's dream alive."[26] Commissioner Doris Noland spoke of Commissioner Kay Rader's leadership: "Kay helped raise awareness of the long drift away from Catherine Booth's ideas on women's ministry." [27]

Despite the advances made under the leadership of the Raders, biblical equality within The Salvation Army, particularly as it relates to gender and ministry, continues to be a goal to be strived for rather than an attainment to be celebrated. It appears to be hampered by factors such as the following:

1. The requirement of officers to be married to other officers (in most territories) and the inherent complications that brings to the appointment process, particularly outside of the corps officer role
2. The positioning of The Salvation Army within an evangelical Western culture that often holds less than egalitarian views
3. The lack of a contemporary articulation of a theology of gender and ministry
4. The lack of role models of (married) women in leadership positions and pulpit ministry
5. A failure to acknowledge the importance of gender-inclusive language in public usage

As a dreamer, I have to raise the question: What could The Salvation Army of the future look like if a tsunami of the Spirit in regards to the model of biblical equality were to roll over me, to roll over the women and men of The Salvation Army, to roll over the structure and the heart of The Salvation Army?

Two New Testament verses highlight the challenge. The first: *"There is no longer Jew nor Greek, there is no longer slave or free, there is no longer male nor female, for all of you are one in Christ Jesus" (Galatians 3:28).* That's the faith component. Now here's the praxis:

> All who believed were together and had all things in common; they would sell their possessions and goods and distribute the proceeds to all, as any had need. Day by day, as they spent much time together in the temple, they broke bread at home and ate their food with glad and generous hearts, praising God and having the goodwill of all the people (Acts 2: 44-46, NRSV).

General Paul Rader understood the challenge: "We must move forward together in all our rich cultural diversity, women and men, the young and the aging and those in mid-life searching for ministry opportunities who will lend their lives new meaning." [28] In a spirit of biblical equality, we must see ourselves as equal in our sin and equal in our redemption, as well as equal in our desire to serve God and equal in our opportunity to serve God. Together, as we live and minister interdependently, with all things in common—resources and power, opportunity and responsibility, strength and weakness—we will continue to shape a Salvation Army that models biblical equality to the world.

Preaching In Millennium 3
"Tell Out the Wonderful Story"

Phil Wall

"Preach the Gospel at all times and if necessary use words." These words, often attributed to Francis of Assisi, could have been written for The Salvation Army. A movement defined by its service to the poor— "Heart to God, Hand to Man" we cry, truly an Army marching on its knees, serving all the way.

However, we are also an Army of preachers, people who from our very inception took seriously the mandate of Scripture articulated clearly by the apostle Paul:

> How then will they call on Him in whom they have not believed? How will they believe in Him whom they have not heard? And how will they hear without a preacher? (Romans 10:14)

On the street, in the village, in the bar room, in the concert hall, in the home and eventually in the Corps building — Salvationists have faithfully been preaching the Gospel for the "whosoever" to whoever will listen.

The Raders are such people — good communicators, insightful, theologically informed, passionate, interesting people, whose lives are driven by authentic faith.

Phil Wall is the CSM at Raynes Park Corps in the London Southeast Division. He met the Raders when first working for the Army as a preaching evangelist in the 1990's and Paul was elected General. They worked together to help design and run the International Youth Forum. Wall reflects, "Their most significant impact on my life and those of my peers was to affirm, trust and support some of the slightly 'edgier' things we were attempting to do. They did this by personal words of affirmation, involving us in their vision, their own preaching and also attending our conference. Their example of humble, godly and holy senior leadership remains the most powerful." Wall's primary role in the salvation war is as an evangelist and he is still most passionate about sharing his faith wherever he can. These days that is primarily within the business community where he spends most of his time running a Leadership Development Company (www.significantleadership.co.uk).

As we honor them in this book I have been asked to reflect on the challenges and capabilities required by those picking up the preaching mantle at the beginning of Millennium 3.

Four themes came to mind that I wanted us to consider.

Biblically Grounded

We live in an age of unprecedented technological change. With computer processing speeds doubling every 18 months, fiber optic cables the width of human hair carrying millions of telephone calls at the same time, marketing executives making business presentations as virtual "Avatars" and a generation growing up who get frustrated if a Google search takes more than micro-seconds, the task of communication is quite a challenging one. The dominant method of preaching is still one individual standing in front of others as a talking head, presenting, uninterrupted, for between 20-30 minutes, whilst on our televisions we will never watch the same image for more than a few seconds.

In such an age, the temptation is to skip the deep rich content of Scripture, aiming to use all sorts of creative devices, anecdotes, and technical wizardry to "entertain" and make a point. Though I confess to having done my fair share of such things, it is not enough today; it has never been enough. People need biblical "meat" and it is the job of the preachers and teachers to provide it. A whole industry has arisen to support churches to share Redemption's story, but this often leaves us lacking in depth. Our talks need to be rich with theological reflection, biblical insight and solid content — we must avoid so much of Western society's addiction to shallow, vacuous content for the sake of expediency.

Please don't hear this as some kind of luddite rant. It is far from it (I am typing this on Apples latest Mac Book Air keyboard). We should use any and every technological tool if it helps us communicate the life-transforming message of Jesus — rather it is a call for faithfulness to Revelation of Depth.

If we are honest with ourselves, the paucity of some of our Salvationist preaching is shocking; shallow homilies will never change the world and those of us entrusted with the task of communication must do the hard yards of preparation and reflection before we open our mouths. We need to be the modern day *"Men of Isaachar, who understood the times and knew what Israel should do"(1 Chronicles 12:32).* We comment and preach to the modern world through the lens of Scripture; there is no Microsoft Windows shortcut to this. No matter how fast Google can give you the address of every Macdonald's in the world, this will always be critical for the preacher.

Authentic

The age of the professional Christian is here — and has been for some time. For those who can say, *"I am paid to follow Jesus, it's my job,"* perils abound to stop us from retaining the authenticity and fire that first drew us to faith. For the professional preacher, teacher, pastor, officer, these challenges are manifold.

Let me highlight just one — withdrawal from "mainstream life." The challenges faced by most in our society cease to become ours as "The Army" pays the bills, etc. Our lives too easily become consumed with the activities of a religious sub-culture that we are paid to service. This means our engagement with real folks in any mode other than service provider or preacher can quickly cease, which is a long way from the missional calling that many responded to.

I am regularly offered the privilege of speaking to Christian leaders, and one of the questions I pose is to ask them the numbers of non-Christian friends they have in their lives. I don't humiliate them by asking for a show of hands but it is clear from the uncomfortable silence that we have touched a raw nerve. As preachers/leaders we often lament the fact that so many of our soldiers seem unable or unwilling to invite their un-churched friends to church. If we look in the mirror, we may well see one of the main reasons why — if we don't they won't.

Preachers who live their lives behind the veil of a religious system often cease to retain their authenticity. Their preaching stories become those they borrow from others, or read in books, as they no longer have any of their own from a life lived in front of a skeptical world. They are starved of such things and thus they, and their preaching, are the poorer for it. We need preachers whose lives are regularly honed and refined by the fires of living faith in a harsh and cynical world. Preachers and leaders, who are able to share their struggles of life and faith with those who do not, have a power, authority and authenticity that can be transformational.

I was on holiday once and noticed that I had a message on my cell phone. As I listened to quite a garbled message from a man who sounded like he was crying uncontrollably, I worked out it was a friend of mine ringing to tell me about his wife who had suddenly been taken critically ill. Towards the end of the call he apologized for troubling me on my holiday and then said words that still give me goose bumps of challenge as I write them now. His closing line was *"Phil, I am so sorry for troubling you, but we need help and you are the only person I know who prays."* Withdrawal is a choice we must avoid at all costs.

Provocative

Catherine Booth (arguably the better preacher of our own dynamic duo) did not mince her words:

> Many do not recognize...that Satan has got men fast asleep in sin. He does not care what we do if he can do that. We may sing songs about the sweet by and by, preach sermons and say prayers until doomsday, and he will never concern himself about us, if we don't wake anybody up. But if we awake the sleeping sinner he will gnash on us with his teeth. This is our work-to wake people up.

Considering the ultra-conservative religious world in which the Army was born, this was powerful stuff. Preachers need to provoke. I may well be biased, but I am pretty sure it is part of our role to stir the soul, disquiet the comfortable and shake the tree of religious pomposity and pretence whenever it is found.

I recall preaching once in a holiness meeting and as I was shaking hands at the door on the way out, I became aware of a man waiting to talk with me. As he did so he made it clear, in words most candid and strident, his disapproval of what he had just heard. To be fair this was quite a regular experience for me, normally because I had been arrogant or insensitive and sometimes because I had just preached badly. If his concerns had been these, I would have probably thought "fair enough." In those early days I remember I had more zeal than holiness or wisdom. However, his complaint was different.

This life long Salvationist complained that my preaching made him and others feel uncomfortable and that he felt my job was not to instigate change but rather to allow people to feel "comfortable" in church. At this point our conversation warmed up a tad and I probably reacted with less maturity than was required or would have been helpful. However, my response then and my response now is the same — no! no! no! Preachers must preach with conviction, with commitment, with passion, and with courage.

On one occasion I was chatting with Kay Rader when she was speaking at one of the early Roots conferences that I was responsible for running in the UK Territory. We were talking about what we were trying to do in challenging the status quo of certain aspects of Army life. As we did so a wry grin came across her face and she said, "I have learned an important lesson in this regard—if you are going to be brave, be very, very brave!" To this day I remain thankful for the challenge of her words.

Preachers need to brave. Part of our role is sometimes to be that prophetic voice that God wants to speak to His people. Sometimes prophets get listened to; sometimes they get stoned. Either way we need to be women and men of courage. The Gospel has power to change lives, situations, communities and so those of us entrusted with platforms must be willing to put our popularity, comfort, ministry careers and reputations on the line to communicate truth with power. If our preaching doesn't regularly stir and if necessary disturb, we must ask God for a fresh revelation to refresh what we preach.

This is one reason why we should be focusing much more energy raising up young preachers. One of the rich legacies of Paul Rader's term as General was the International Youth Forum in Cape Town in 1997. The entire tone and purpose was to empower and give voice to a whole generation of young Salvationists. The impact of this event is still felt nearly 20 years on through the relationships and programs that emerged from it. It gave permission for young people to be brave, experiment, and chase their Kingdom inspired dreams.

Today, those of us who preach should also be looking to raise up and mentor young "provocative" preachers. You know you are listening to one when you draw in a sharp breath and say to yourself, *"I wouldn't say it like that"* and wince with pain. The history of the church, and certainly this movement, has often been shaped by the power of provocative words uttered by young prophets whose maturity and elegance is someway behind their pronouncements. But God uses them anyway and we established preachers have a responsibility to seek out and mentor these young firebrands. When the prophets are quiet the church should quake.

Holiness

Thomas Celeno, a biographer of Assisi, writing three years after Francis's death, quotes his instructions for fellow preachers:

> The preacher must first draw from secret prayers what he will later pour out in holy sermons; he must first grow hot within before he speaks words that are in themselves cold.

The life of holiness for a preacher is one in which *"growing hot within"* needs to be a regular discipline. I feel shame as I recall the times I have preached with a cold heart, unstirred by the message, unchanged by its power, delivering with reasonable skill but lacking the authority that only comes from the unction of the Spirit. Sadly, I am not alone.

We should regularly recall the fact that so often when Jesus or the apostles actually did anything that we would remotely call "preaching" it was as an explanation of an extraordinary Spirit empowered event or miracle. Where is the demonstration of power in our lives and preaching? Where do we see God at work in miraculous ways, changing lives, changing us? If you are a preacher or leader reading this and your response to what you just read was one of cynicism, dismissal, or exasperation at my naivety feel free to stop reading—what follows will only frustrate you more. On the other hand you could do what I did as I reflected on my life as a preacher: get on your knees, weep and repent of what you have done with His holy calling on your life. Ask Him to refresh and renew, to reinvigorate your passion for the lost, your hunger for His word and your thirst for His Spirit and thus the power of your preaching. There is no other way.

As a young Salvationist I grew cynical of Youth Council appeals, aiming to recruit candidates for officership that seemed to aim to grind you down by singing the chorus "To Be Like Jesus" about 30 times. In more recent years I have returned to the song and its sentiment. In short it is a prayer no doubt prayed regularly by the Raders in their rich ministry; it is also the prayer needing to be prayed daily by the preachers of Millennium 3.

To be like Jesus!
This hope possesses me,
In every thought and deed,
This is my aim, my creed;
To be like Jesus!
This hope possesses me,
His Spirit helping me,
Like him I'll be.

Integrity

"All My Work is for the Master"

Herbert Rader

A taxi driver returns a briefcase left behind; an employee works even harder during the boss's absence; a driver assumes personal responsibility for damage caused to another car in a parking lot. But at the same time a man receiving total disability payments is discovered leading a martial arts class, and the CEO of a charitable organization for impoverished members of his religious community pockets a million dollars of public support money!

Stealing at work and cheating in school are commonplace. Term papers are downloaded wholesale, and trusted journalists fabricate stories. Prosecutors withhold evidence and defense attorneys deceive juries without regard to guilt or innocence. Professors reject findings that contradict long-held opinions. It does not seem to be a world in which there is a serious concern about ultimate truth.

How destructive to individuals, organizations and society is a lack of integrity, when trust is betrayed, or things are not as they are claimed or thought to be! Unfortunately, fraudulent damage or disability claims, inflated expense accounts, exaggerated deductions on IRS returns, or deliberate lies by parents who feign illness, drain the meaning from "integrity," and train the next generation to compromise the truth.

On a recent tour of our town we admired our elegant Centennial Hall with its four tall pillars and capitals that appear to be supporting a stately, faux-Grecian pediment.

Paul Rader and his wife Lois have soldiered at the Hempstead Corps in the Greater New York Division since 1984, and have both been involved in the Sunday School program most of that time. Herb reflects, "My parents, Lyell and Gladys Rader, were a powerful influence on the family, teaching and demonstrating that life must be Christ-centered, service oriented, Bible-based and Spirit controlled." These Raders served as medical missionaries in India for 12 years, and since returning to the U.S. in 1983, he has served as medical director of three New York hospitals, finally retiring at age 75.

Alas, we discovered that the base of one pillar was completely rotted through, and was clearly not supporting anything.

Integrity is not just the decorative façade of a structure, but its essential foundation — the girders that support the entire building! Integrity in construction means that the beams will not break, the joints will not come apart, the concrete will not disintegrate, the elevators will not fall, the wiring will not short circuit and the plumbing will not leak.

Termites can eat wooden support timbers in a house and conceal their presence and activity until the floor gives way! When things are not as they should be — when short cuts have been taken, shoddy work has been done and sub-standard materials have been used, it not only reflects the lack of integrity of the builders, but it causes a lack of integrity of the structure. There is a deep lack of wholeness.

But integrity is vital in many domains: we look for and depend upon integrity in political affairs; we depend upon the integrity of organizations. We depend upon integrity in business. We certainly expect integrity in science and in medicine. And it almost goes without saying that we insist upon integrity in personal relationships — keeping one's vows, keeping one's word.

There was a day when a man who said, "Upon my honor," or "I give you my word," could be counted upon to keep his pledge without recourse to contracts and lawyers.

There is no question that our entire society is structured on integrity. What if military contractors did not build according to specification? What if cancer medications did not actually contain the ingredients on the label? What if real estate valuations or engineering reports were inaccurate? What if the materials used in tunnels and bridges were defective? Society would literally collapse.

Integrity means that claims are backed up, commitments are honored; promises are kept. We do not hide in disclaimers; we do not look for loopholes, we do not hope the customer will not look too closely.

Any person, church, organization or nation that loses its integrity is on the way to ruin. When lying, stealing, cheating and dissembling, are rampant, the heart of the entity is sick with a condition that will eventually prove fatal.

Arul Dhas, a Salvationist from a small village in south India, served as hospital accountant for many years at the Army's Catherine Booth Hospital. On one occasion he spent an entire night laboring over the ledgers to find a missing penny, while at the same time another employee, serving as hospital cashier, found to his delight and profit that the cash register was not taping everything that was put into the drawer and that the excess could be pocketed without detection.

The infamous "O" ring that caused a billion dollar NASA project to end in disaster demonstrates how important the small parts are to a large undertaking. A small, inexpensive ring that sealed a solid booster rocket failed just after the launch of the Space Shuttle Challenger in 1986, and seven astronauts lost their lives. So much depends upon the integrity of the whole system.

Integrity means "as advertised." Claims made are fulfilled; promises are kept and convictions are honored when the pressure is on. For the Christian, integrity means making choices that are aligned with God's will, and inviting God's scrutiny of our actions and motives.

The trouble is that we grow out of innocence and naiveté into a kind of cynicism that we consider "grown up" in a world of competition, struggle for survival, compromise and conflict, where cutting corners and reinterpreting contract terms and backing out of treaty agreements are just part of doing "business."

The history of diplomacy is a sad chronicle or saga of duplicity, illegal intelligence gathering and espionage, creating crises to further agendas, and playing real or potential adversaries off against each other. It is a world of intrigue rather than integrity.

Why do we have to preface our remarks with "to tell you the truth," or "honestly," or "to be honest with you," or "I swear," etc. What does that say about unprefaced statements?

Like the tensile strength of the nylon rope firmly fixed to the climber's belt ready to arrest his fall in the event of a slip, so integrity reveals itself in the moment of crisis to save the man who has it. When our desires and motivations accord with our values and beliefs, and these two inner coordinates are consistent with our habits and intention and spontaneous behavior, we are acting with integrity.

The Cynic Diogenes was an eccentric character in the age of the great Greek philosophers, who gained a reputation for roaming the streets with a lamp, claiming to be looking for "one honest person." The prophet Jeremiah questions whether there is actually anyone who seeks the truth and suggests that it will be hard to find in the human heart!

In the Information Technology world, two words have great importance: compromise and integrity. The latter means that the software is working reliably as programmed without corruption of data. Compromise means that the system has been taken over by something false, security has been breached, there has been critical system failure, and the output cannot be trusted!

Integrity is having a solid foundation of faith, and clear guidelines for living with well demarcated boundaries. There may be some reasonable accommodation, but the man of integrity knows where the "red lines" are and will not cross them, even to avoid the furnace. The man of integrity says, "I stand before God to whom I must give an account," and I will not do it!"

We can be so well supported and so closely observed that any breach of integrity would require CIA tradecraft. But integrity is demonstrated when we are left to our own devices in a lonely outpost where we have authority without accountability, or when we are thrust into the limelight or a place of honor, or when we are kept under intense, unrelenting, exhausting stress. Only God can expose our weakness and reveal his strength in us!

Meanwhile, integrity must reflect a solid core built of a desire to please God in each successive challenge in calm or storm, rather than the result of personal efforts that foster pride. Indeed, when all seems to be well we may discover to our grief the emergence of pride, the ever-lurking self-satisfaction, the enemy of all spiritual good. Pharisees kept the letter of the law very well while misunderstanding its purpose.

Is it not true that outstanding individuals — people of integrity — who are designated as spiritual leaders and given ego-inflating titles and authority may discover how difficult it is to escape the disqualifying grip of pride? It is possible, but only for those who regularly endure true humbling experiences and unceasing Spirit-guided pruning and discipline.

Integrity is not gleaming veneer; it is the stuff we are made of; it is the core that continues to show through even when the surface is deeply scarred. It is a quality of mind and spirit that struggles and grieves and repents over the realities of the heart and seeks continuous cleansing and refining by the Holy Spirit.

The "persona" was the stage mask in the Greek theater, carefully positioned to prevent breaking the prescribed illusion. Persons advised to "just be yourself," may respond, "which self?" We are all capable of accepting roles like costumes, sometimes passed along by a predecessor.

One may legitimately grow in a position, but it is not healthy to allow the position to shape one in a way that is inauthentic and that requires Wizard of Oz like pretense. The projection of an idealized self may be a strategy for concealing a darker interior reality. How easy to become trapped in lifelong delusion.

Integrity is not another word for perfection, but integrity means that we not only tell the truth in our dealings with others, but we listen to the truth about ourselves and grieve when we fail.

Recently some politicians, exposed in embarrassing personal scandals, have made claims about their integrity based on their partial and forced admissions, with no evidence of repentance or change of heart. Public comment was measured and guarded. There was no sign of true sorrow or grief.

The trouble is that in positions of power, we are likely to bring in consultants and legal advisers to defend our position or actions when it would be better to hire the storybook character who finally identified the inadequacy of the emperor's attire.

People of integrity live in a "no spin zone." It is a narrow space— an unobstructed corridor of truth telling without obfuscation, rationalization and misleading half-truths. It is a Spirit-inhabited space where increasing Spirit control and increasing love of truth result in increasing integrity.

The great friend of integrity is genuine humility — saying about ourselves what God says; an enemy of integrity is pharisaical pride in one's own strength, wisdom, or performance.

Integrity requires not only that we tell and live the truth, but that we face the truth even when it is disturbing. It is common to have selective hearing when exposed to truth that exposes a false position we may hold. One professor's pride prevented him from correcting his curriculum even after he discovered it was wrong. Let God be true and every man a liar!

In any conversation about integrity, someone is likely to recall some event in their past that makes them feel uneasy. I'm confident that honest reflection will turn up some attitude or action that failed the integrity standard and required repentance.

One should certainly not claim to be what he or she is not. At the same time one must press on whole-heartedly to achieve the level of integrity which family and organization and society and God have every right to expect.

Integrity is a matter of the heart. We may never be perfect in performance. We may never achieve absolute consistency. But like the very human and flawed David, who was a man after God's own heart, we may claim integrity, as David so often does in his personal diaries, when our hearts truly desire to do and to be what is right in God's sight, and when there is profound humility and deep repentance when we fail.

It is difficult to be perfectly consistent all the time in every situation, but it is God who is at work in the life of the sincere believer both to will and to do of his good pleasure. We need a principle within to align disparate inclinations, and to bring body mind and spirit into harmony, the harmony seen so clearly in the life of the Lord Jesus.

It is likely to be the work of a lifetime to bring every errant thought and action under the control and purging influence of the Holy Spirit.

Even Paul made no claims to have arrived at a place of perfection, but he was certainly a man of unimpeachable integrity. It was his highest goal to know Jesus and to be with him and to be like him in whom there was no falsehood! (John 7:18). Paul's resources are available to us! Search my heart, O God. (Psalm 139:23-24).

Never! The GEN Y Cry

"Arise, O Youth"

Joe Noland

T he story is legend. William Booth, appalled by the broken sea of humanity sleeping beneath the London Bridge, turned to his son, Bramwell, and said, "DO SOMETHING!" For Booth, this was a frantic cry to reach what he called "the submerged tenth." It was a call to go and be the church, as modeled by Jesus and his early day followers. "Go to where the people are to be got at!"

Culture Changes

Time goes by and culture changes. The world is shrinking because of technology, bringing instant access to the masses globally. That submerged tenth has exploded exponentially as the population has sextupled over the past century. Here's a statistic that will boggle the mind, taken from globalissues.org: "Out of 2.2 billion children in the world, 1 billion live in poverty (every second child = submerged fiftieth). The distance between the richest and poorest countries catapulted from 3 to 1 in 1820, to 72 to 1 in 1992. And this is but a small sampling.

Time goes by and church culture changes. With each passing generation we grow more contented, snuggling into the warm, safe environs of our sanctuaries, almost womblike, protective and nonthreatening.

See Bio under "Genesis" chapter above. In addition, Noland is retired, now fully engaged in the "no strings attached" creative process. His ministry can be summed up in three words: Chaos, Creativity and Controversy—three elements implicit in any successful innovative endeavor. As Noland says often, "Creativity is my drug of choice."

We soothe our consciences by increasing our missionary giving largely, raising millions to build the latest state-of-the-art treatment facilities, youth centers and family shelters, inviting the submerged "however many" in without going out... and getting our hands dirty. This writer pleads guilty, a product of the silent, contented generation.

NEVER!

And then a new generation burst upon the scene, GEN Y (Millennials 18-29), as some bright writer has labeled them — 2.5 billion strong worldwide. *NEVER!* is their hue and cry. "We don't want a church that entertains us on weekends, performance art, video technology and all. We don't want to entertain mission; we want to engage mission. We don't want to simply contribute financially to a cause; we want to be consumed completely by the cause, get our hands dirty, step out on the edge, be missionaries right in our own backyards wherever they may be. This is how we want to worship. We're looking for mission, a movement, like the Army of yore!"

The church has turned a deaf ear to that hue and cry, and this generation is deserting the church as if it were a sinking ship. This is not meant to be a scientific treatise, but rather an essay based upon research and experience. A recent Pew Research Study concludes that,

> By some key measures, Americans ages 18 to 29 are considerably less religious than older Americans. Compared with their elders today, young people are much less likely to affiliate with any religious tradition or identify themselves as part of a Christian denomination... Yet not belonging does not necessarily mean not believing.

Involved in a Cause!

This same study, however, describes a generation that is "Confident, Connected and Open to Change." There are 79 million Millennials (in America). Ryan Scott, Founder and CEO Causecast writes, "So if employers want to hold on to this demographic, they must implement employee retention practices that speak to Gen Y. Many of those practices are rooted in one thing — CAUSE."

"A recent Boston Consulting Group study found that Millennials are concerned about big social issues and believe that involvement in causes is a fundamental part of life." Substitute the words, "employers" above with "church" or "The Salvation Army," and "employee retention" with "church" or "Salvation Army retention," and the way forward becomes quite clear. Get them involved in a cause!

To my knowledge, there have been no Salvation Army specific studies regarding diminishing returns within this age group, but it is statistically and experientially acknowledged that an inordinate amount of young people leave the Army during these crucial years.

Revolution Hawaii

Fortunately, there are those spiritually attuned to the hue and cry, with GEN Y age specific mission stations beginning to establish themselves and spread across the Army world. I'm most conversant with a USA Western Territory expression, Revolution Hawaii. Rob and Denise Noland are its visionary pioneers.

Reaching this generation is their passion, and through them I have become spiritually attuned. Revolution Hawaii's vision and mission is to reverse the trends alluded to above, and to capture and disciple young adults so that, instead of leaving the church (Army) they will instead embrace the church (Army). remaining passionately engaged in its mission and ministry.

Get them involved in a cause! Young adults (18-29) are recruited from throughout the USA Western Territory, and beyond, sacrificially committing to a mission immersion experience, incarnationally — social action, evangelism, Bible study and prayer rounding out the curriculum.

Home base is Camp Homelani (Heavenly Home) on the North Shore of Oahu, Hawaii. From here the team reaches out to the uttermost and nether most. Following are Mission Tracks presently available (A work in progress):

1. 365: "A Year to Change A Lifetime!"
2. Essentials: A 3-month "taste" of what Revolution Hawaii is all about, a great place to start, offered twice a year in September

and February.

3. Missions: A 3-month missions program in the Federated States of Micronesia and The Marshall Islands, offered 3 times a year, October, February and June.

4. Summer Camp: A specialized track for those interested in becoming part of the summer camping mission experience.

5. Surf: An opportunity to surf and serve in "The Surf Capitol of the World," while learning to live, love and serve like Jesus.

6. Other: Nehemiah (Recovery), Creative Arts, etc., in their creative stages.

Two equally spiritually attuned, ardent supporters of RevHi's vision and mission are General Paul and Commissioner Kay Rader, and they have the distinction of being made honorary Revolution Hawaii team members. Although of another generation, they really *get it!*

Roger

"Go to where the people are to be got at. Do something!" Fast-forward 125 years. The Revolution Hawaii team had just spent two nights living homeless on the mean streets of Honolulu. Here they met Roger, a partially paralyzed drunk, long scraggily, matted down hair and beard, looking far older than his birth age, his life spent atop a flattened cardboard box, begging for change to feed his habit.

"The first time I met Roger" recounts Rob Noland, Director of Revolution Hawaii, "he was being carried into our Upper Room service by team members who placed him on one of the front row pews. The smell was overpowering, causing everyone to move far back into the chapel, except for those few brave team members, sitting with arms around him so that he wouldn't feel alone. Scrounging up a battered wheelchair, they wheeled him back week after week."

DO SOMETHING!

Five years earlier, Roger had been in a fight, leading to bleeding in the brain, which led to a stroke paralyzing the right side of his body. This resulted in a deep depression and a conscious decision to drink himself to death. Consequently, unable to get to a bathroom, he defecated and urinated in his clothing, never having the opportunity to bathe or shower. This is how they found him every week.

He loved coming to Upper Room, followed by fellowship downstairs where dinner was served and food prepared for street evangelism and outreach following. One evening he commented that the lasagna Ernie Ing bought at Sam's Club was "the best home-made lasagna I have ever tasted!"

DO SOMETHING!

The 5th week Roger expressed a desire to get into a clean and sober house. John, one of the RevHi team members, took him to the dorms, personally bathing, shaving and outfitting him with a set of clean clothes. Following, he looked 15-years younger, a newfound glow about him. He began to open up about his life, originally coming to Hawaii to work on geo thermal wells, married, divorced, children and grandchildren.

Following the stroke, he lost his job, apartment, and girlfriend, spiraling into depression, addiction and a futile sense of hopelessness. DO SOMETHING! reverberating down through the centuries, now being echoed in the ministry of Revolution Hawaii and Upper Room.

Through the team's efforts, Roger was accepted into a clean and sober house. Fast-forward five months. His badly infected foot is healed; he walks with a cane, is of clear speech and praising God joyfully. He leads AA and NA meetings and is looking forward to being reunited with his children and grandchildren—a living, breathing, redemptive 21st century trophy of grace. SAVN.tv (Salvation Army Vision Network) captured Roger telling his story on film, and can be viewed by copying the following into an Internet browser: http://savn.tv/campaign/view/1070

One corps officer, in her recommendation on the application of a recent team member, writes, "I know this will change her life. The last three that came through RevHI from my corps jumped right into ministry when they returned. Hoping the same for this one, hate to lose her as a soldier, but want her to come forward as a leader."

This officer's hope, "come forward as a leader," sums up the vision and purpose of Revolution Hawaii. For a more comprehensive look, copy this link into your Internet browser: www.revolutionhawaii.com.

This emerging generation is the Present Future
"Confident, Connected, Open to Change"

Partners In Mission
"Help Us To Help Each Other, Lord"

Bronwyn and Lyndon Buckingham

Recently Bronwyn and I visited a small village in Myanmar. The village is a forty-five minute drive from Yangon. It is basic to say the least and yet at the same time has an amazing appeal. We were there to share in worship with the corps folk of the "Lay Daung Khan Corps." The hall turned out to be the front room of a small house owned by the husband of one of the soldiers of the corps. We arrived to find it packed full of smiling, uniformed Salvationists of all ages. There was a sense of anticipation, of joy and fun and, in a way, we could tell the Lord had already shown up and was enjoying the praise of His people. The personal circumstances of these wonderful people was clearly meager, yet their riches in Christ Jesus, clearly evident and truly inspirational.

By some measures they possessed a great deal less than Bronwyn and I, yet on another level, it seemed to me they had so much more. A depth of spirituality, an awareness of the presence of the King of Kings and a humble yet determined desire to testify and praise Him for all His goodness. We were there to bless them, but as we partnered with them in worship and ministry on that hot Sunday morning, we found ourselves being ministered to. As we worshipped the Lord together we found ourselves drawn into the presence of the King in a very special way.

Bronwyn and Lyndon Buckingham are soldiers of the Changi Corps in Singapore where they serve as territorial leaders of Singapore, Malaysia, and Myanmar. They first met the Raders during a campaign in their home territory, New Zealand, Fiji, and Tonga, in the late 1990s, and have admired the Raders' passion, vision, and integrity. The Buckinghams have been impacted by the Raders' passion and articulate communication of the Gospel. As far as claims to fame, they are loved by God so much that He sent His Son for them. They are children of God!

It was a wonderful reminder to us "that where two or three are gathered in His name"...! and His presence was more than enough. As I watched Bronwyn sharing the Gospel with our brothers and sisters on that wonderful Sunday, I was taken back to the Chapel at Booth College of Mission in New Zealand. The scene unfolding in my mind was our Covenant Day Service back in January 1990. We were kneeling at the mercy seat to sign our officer covenant. We prayed together on that significant day. "If we are going to do this, let's do it together!" We have been partnering in mission and ministry ever since. Little did we foresee that commitment would take us all the way to a small village in Myanmar to worship with brothers and sisters in Christ. Our partnership in mission has provided us with countless opportunities to share the love of Jesus, using our combined gifts and skills to minister and serve others.

Bronwyn

It has been quite the journey as we have learned to work together using our various gifts and talents to partner in mission as we serve Christ and the Army. Lyndon is the visionary, the big picture guy, full of ideas and possibilities and the next big project. Sometimes I wonder where the ideas come from and quite honestly some need to be lost as soon as they are discovered! I love the fact that he is always seeing new possibilities and in his mind, nothing is ever a problem. As for me, I am more of a planner, a detailer, the organizer if you will. Give me a list and a time line and I am a "happy camper." As we have come to appreciate and value what we each bring to the table, so we have been able to better partner together for the sake of the mission. We are better together, that's for sure. Actually what is true for a married couple working together in partnership is true for any team however it is comprised, who want to achieve something for the Kingdom. Appreciating each other's gifts and skill mix and partnering together can have wonderful results.

What a blessing it has been to our marriage and ministry not to be in competition with each other but rather to partner together for the Gospel. We are so grateful to God and the Army for giving us amazing opportunities to share our love for Jesus with others in the hope they will choose to follow Him as well.

Lyndon

I am discovering more and more the strength and power of partnering in the Gospel. Jesus sent his disciples out in pairs. Paul, as much as he could, had people with him on his missionary journeys. I think we should partner more. Think of the possibilities. What about two or three corps families partnering together to reach another family for Jesus. What about members of a youth group joining up to reach one other young person and then repeating the exercise. What about corps working together to take a neighborhood for Jesus. Territories working together, partnering to take new ground for the Kingdom. Partnering works. Patch, power and politics will destroy any mission initiative. But co-operating, partnering and sharing resources around a common goal releases so much energy and excitement and the outcomes are so often beyond what had been expected or hoped for.

Lay Daung Khan Corps was given "corps status" in May 2013. Despite the fact that they don't have their own hall and resources are limited, they are already partnering with a village down the road. They want to start an outpost and are working together with their corps officer to get it off the ground. I have no doubt lives will be transformed as a result.

I found myself thanking God for the privilege of shared ministry as I watched Bronwyn share the love of Jesus from her heart on that Sunday morning. Eyes bright, smile wide, cheeks rosy from the heat. Willing her translator (another form of partnering) on so she could get out the next sentence. Eager listeners affirming her with smiles and "amens" as the message was understood. I am sure the Lord was smiling on our humble efforts. Doing ministry together is an awesome privilege and such a blessing.

The Raders exemplified shared ministry and the power of partnering for the Gospel. We, with others, celebrate their mission hearts, worldwide contribution and ongoing ministry. We thank God for the impact and influence of their lives on countless others. We are thankful for the way God continues to use them to grow His Kingdom.

The Gospels record a story of a young boy who once partnered with Jesus. John's Gospel (John 9) records for us this special event. Many had gathered to hear Jesus, it was getting late in the day and Jesus was keen to have the people fed. This sent the disciples into a tailspin. "Eight months wages would not be enough to feed all these people." The task was overwhelming, or seemingly so anyway.

Andrew brought a young boy who was prepared to offer his small lunch to Jesus. Nice moment, but really, one small lunch is hardly going to solve the challenge, is it? Unless you remember who the young boy is partnering with. He brought what he had to Jesus. Jesus, the King of kings and Lord of Lords. The result of this unlikely partnership is described as a miracle. Potentially we are all partners in mission. Bringing what we are and have to the master, Jesus, partnering with Him for the salvation of the world. It seems to me that when we are talking about partnering, we dare not forget to include the master, Jesus.

If The Salvation Army is to have an effective future as an instrument in the hands of God, we must find ways, new ways, creative ways, out of the box ways to partner with Him and each other for the sake of the mission. It is our conviction that the collective resources of God's Salvation Army provides a platform for some incredible partnering so that we might reach the furthest corners of the globe with the love of God and the transforming power of Jesus. There are neighborhoods all around the world that are just waiting for some energized, partnered up Salvationists to show up and share their lunch. What are you waiting for?

Legacy

"We're the Army That Shall Conquer"

Freda and John Larsson

When the gigantic tsunami wave recedes from the shores it has battered it leaves behind a transformed landscape. In the case of a tsunami the force is destructive—it brings ruination in its wake. But when the tsunami of the Spirit rolls over God's people it is the most creative force in the universe at work, and it leaves behind it a world where everything is new and beautiful.

In the late 19th century when the tsunami of the Spirit smashed over a struggling movement called The Christian Mission it left in its wake a shiny new, marvelous and unique creation called The Salvation Army. "We're the Army that shall conquer," sang the Salvationists of the day. And this newborn Army swept everything before it. Thank God for this legacy of the Spirit!

It was a marvelous legacy! The creative energies let loose by the tsunami of the Spirit from 1878 to the end of that century were staggering. From nothing came a new creation that within a few years had swept across the world. And permanence was implanted into the creation by a vast production of written material that, like an enormous satellite photo, captures every detail of the Army as it was at that time.

This aerial picture of what the tsunami of the Spirit created in the final decades of the 19th century is a precious part of our legacy as a movement.

Freda and John Larsson soldier at Bromley Temple Corps, South London, UK. They first met the Raders when moving into territorial leadership, both at roughly the same time. In their words, "The Raders have been an example of intellectual distinction combining with down-to-earth front-line service." John invests his time in writing books and articles, well known as half of the Gowan/Larsson "Musical" team. Freda gave 25 years of service to women's ministries as an active officer, and when she retired served as the corps home league secretary for seven years. John Larsson was the 20th Chief of the Staff and 17th General of The Salvation Army.

Nothing can detract from the amazing things the Spirit did at that time. We are right to go back to that picture again and again to examine it closely in order to discern what the core values are that are permanent and will always remain.

But looking back, whether to those glorious times at the end of the 19th century or just to more recent yesterdays, has its dangers. By keeping on looking back to discern the future, we may miss the greatest of all legacies that the Spirit has bequeathed to the Army. And this is that the waters of the Spirit have never stopped rolling over the Army. Our greatest legacy is not what the Spirit created in the past but the fact that the Spirit has never stopped his creative activity in and through the Army.

Drawing inspiration from what the Spirit did in the past and drawing stimulus from what he is doing in the present are both necessary in our evolution as a movement. There will always be a degree of tension between the two concepts, but as befits an Army born of a tsunami of the Spirit, succeeding generations of Salvationists have usually managed to find a balance between the two legacies.

We see that balance in the way the Army has taken root in different countries. When in its earliest days the Army spread out from its birth country of England, the original vision of the pioneers was to replicate as far as possible what the tsunami of the Spirit had created in Britain. But fortunately the early pioneers were also alive to the legacy of a Spirit who is always creating something new. And from that blend of legacies came that glorious mixture which is the international Salvation Army — an Army which is recognizably the same everywhere and yet is truly distinctive from country to country.

In India, to take a dramatic example, pioneer Frederick Tucker had no hesitation in discarding most of what he had seen in England. He realized that if the Army was to take root in so different a culture it had to be a different Army. "The adoption of Indian food, dress, names and customs," records The Salvation Army Year Book, "gave the pioneers ready access to the people, especially in the villages." And yet it was essentially the same Army as back in England. Similarly, adaptations of some kind or other have been made in all countries to which the Army has been transplanted.

But every territory will have its own stories of the creative tension there has been over the years in determining how much of the original British vision to retain and how much to adapt to local culture. And local historians will argue for many years to come how right each country got it.

As the Army's international leaders, General Paul A. Rader and Commissioner Kay F. Rader experienced first hand everywhere they travelled the miracle of the one and same yet different Army. But after their many years in Korea, where the Army has with remarkable success managed to combine the original vision with Korean culture, nothing they saw as the world leaders will have come as a surprise to them.

Each individual country will also have experienced the creative tension there is between those wanting to keep what the tsunami of the Spirit created in the past in that country and those who want to discern what the Spirit wants to create today. How easy it is to forget that the creative tension is meant to find its resolution in the combination of the two legacies.

This tension has been seen in many areas. Many battles have been fought over the uniform—and its style. At one time it was all about the bonnet. Said some: if the bonnet goes it is the end of the Army. Fortunately the Army was open to new revelation on that point as on so many more.

Then there were the worship wars that raged in some countries between those advocating the new praise and worship songs sung off the wall, and those insisting that songs must be Army and sung from the song book. How good that when it comes to music the Army seems to have learned that a balance of the traditional and contemporary, the old and the new, the classic and the Army, is the only way for the vast riches of God's gift to his people to be fully used.

The creative tension between the traditional and the new has also been felt in the realm of mission. The original vision for evangelical ministry was enshrined in *Orders and Regulations for Field Officers* published in 1886—the finest handbook on corps work that the Army has ever published. The original pattern for social mission was encapsulated in William Booth's *In Darkest England and the*

Way Out published in 1890. As the Army spread around the world each territory had to decide how much of this original vision could be adapted to local circumstances.

But with the passage of time the Army in each country has also faced the ever-present danger of its evangelical and social mission getting into a rut. Outer circumstances keep changing, and it is easy for a movement to find itself meeting the needs of yesterday rather than those of today. How indebted we are to prophets who have opened our eyes to see new challenges and opportunities.

Paul A. Rader and Kay F. Rader have been cast in that prophetic role. When in Korea, God used them in a remarkable way to implant a new vision of evangelism and growth in that country. While leaders of the USA Western Territory they caught the imagination of Salvationists by the boldness of the MISSION 2000 concept. And no one present at the High Council at which the then Commissioner Paul A. Rader was elected General will forget his visionary words about the Army's mission:

We must go forward in finding cost-effective, supportable means for entering new areas of ministry... forward in compassionate and creative response to the AIDS pandemic... forward in our efforts to find and enfold the lost and then enlist them in our great cause... forward in aggressive and innovative approaches to evangelism...forward in our efforts to sensitize and mobilize our people to confront the moral crises in our communities... forward in our commitment as an Army—east and west, north and south—to world evangelization.

Those words had a direct bearing on what followed. As the official History of The Salvation Army records, Paul A. Rader was elected unanimously by the High Council—the only General to have achieved this distinction.

Thank God for the prophets of every generation who have made the Army alive to its legacy of continual renewal by the Spirit.

When the early Salvationists looked around them and saw the transformation that the tsunami of the Spirit was creating, how right they were to sing "We're the Army that shall conquer!" We praise God for the inspiration, which that legacy has been to every succeeding generation of Salvationists.

But we also praise God that the Army has not lived on that legacy alone but has also been open to the legacy of continual re-creation by the Spirit. Through that legacy we know that the Spirit will never cease to roll over His Army, and, if we let Him, will never cease to keep creating a Salvation Army that shall conquer!

Conclusion??

Stephen Court

Since General Rader called Salvationists to prayer in 1994 enjoining us to cry out to God for a tsunami of the Spirit that has been a daily phrase in my conversations with God.

And we give God glory for answers to that prayer, multiplied millions of times by a "million marching" over the days and years of spiritual war.

Groundswells of the Holy Spirit in certain regions of the earth have brought renown to our great God Yahweh. People have encountered the Spirit of the Lord Jesus Christ in dreams while asleep as our Savior bypasses cultural and religious religious barriers to save lost people.

Holy Spirit upsurges have renewed and refreshed stagnant parts of the Body of Christ, reflecting splendor to our marvelous King and Redeemer as reinvigorated disciples have flexed atrophied systems to exercise the power of God in our midst.

There has even been a welling up of Holy Spirit awareness and saturation in the West as Jesus' followers are growing more and more convinced that life and war-fighting in the 21st century is at best a pedestrian proposition without His embrace (and if you can't keep up with the foot soldiers, how will you compete with the horses? Jeremiah 12:5) — this, too, exalts our Lord.

Every surge of the Holy Spirit, in conversion, in sanctification, in healing, in deliverance, in restoration, in miracles, in reconciliation, in anointing, in calling, in commissioning, in comforting – builds faith, bests the enemy, and burnishes God's glory.

Global Tsunami

And yet, in all honesty, we're looking for much more. We're hanging on for something much greater. We're anticipating a global tsunami. We're praying for it. We're fighting for it. We're believing in it.

We do not settle for "making a difference," "leaving a legacy," "being an influence." We're wanting God's boundless salvation to sweep the earth with wave after wave of Holy Spirit love and purity and power, the whole world redeeming.

Life-Long Tsunami

The Raders' lives have been a generational story of Tsunami, Holy Spirit rolling in and through them in transformative, creative energy, sometimes following, though God is not limited, the four stages of tsunami formation.

The initiation stage has been recounted in their biography, and a bit more in these pages, as spiritual kinetic energy set life's direction and callings in motion.

And there have been splitting stages as well, chaos and crisis, as calling and opportunity seemed at odds, as appointment and passion seemed in conflict. But God was stirring through these challenges, refining character, firming resolve, and crafting strategy to attack the enemy on these very fronts.

And they know first-hand the amplification stage as Holy Spirit amplitude increases, resulting in a steepening of the wave. They know the uncertainty of dynamic change, the human insecurity of supernatural tumult.

And, glory to God, the Raders have seen on several occasions, in Korea, in the western United States, and internationally, the run up stage that features a rapid rise in spiritual sea level. They've known Holy Spirit run up.

General Bramwell Booth on holiness: "If holiness is possible anywhere for anyone at anytime, it is possible anywhere for everyone at all times." To paraphrase him, if a Tsunami of the Spirit is possible in Korea or the Western States for the Raders in the 70s and the 90s, it is possible anywhere for everyone at all times.

If so, how?

The chapters of this book have explored different features of the Raders' lives. Not all of their beliefs or emphases or experiences are essential for a Tsunami of the Spirit. We all don't have to have been raised from the dead when a baby (like Commissioner Kay) or to have been what we'd see today as a trans-denominational professional worship leader in college days (like General Paul) to see a Tsunami of the Spirit. We all don't have to have studied at Asbury, learned Korean, or advocate Pure Hope (see purehope.net, for which General Paul serves on the Board). But it sure might help to embrace covenant, champion egalitarianism, exhibit holiness, exercise vision, risk goals, model evangelistic fervor, submit to Scripture, lead by example, stand for justice, disciple the next generation, epitomize salvationism, display holy boldness and show integrity.

There are some mandatories. [29]

We need to be saved. That is, we need to have accepted Jesus' invitation into His life when He offered, "Come, follow Me" (Mark 1:17). Those of us who are saved will have repented and believed (Mark 1:15). Instead of trying to shrink the Savior of the universe into our tiny lives, we obey His call — Come, follow Me — and become a part of His gigantic, supernatural, history-making, eternity-shaking life. So, rather than ignore, stall, compromise, or straight-up reject this amazing invitation / command, and end up in a different post-mortem destination, the best decision we can ever make is to follow Jesus, submitting to His Lordship in our lives.

We need to be free. The Raders are involved with Pure Hope, a movement envisioning a world free of sexual exploitation and brokenness. So many are bound by habitual sin, even beyond the sexual. And many of these addictions are imposed and exploited by demonic forces. We needn't be demonized as followers of the Lord Jesus Christ. After all, disobedient angels are chained in darkness until judgment (Jude 6). The key for us is not to give the devil a foothold (Ephesians 4:27), any space of darkness — any unconfessed sin—in which demons have freedom of movement. If we repent and renounce these sins we will be forgiven and the darkness will be swept away by light and we can authoritatively command demons to leave and go where Jesus sends them.

And we need to be sanctified. We can be entirely sanctified, right now. The person who is completely consecrated — every area of your life; the person who is completely confessed up — every sin that God identifies; the person who is completely confident — sure that God in His goodness enables what He commands and commands us to be holy — that person can be sanctified through and through, right now.

Don't worry... Your Father delights to give you the kingdom (Luke 12:32). Saved, freed, holy people are positioned down-current in the ocean of God's grace, positioned for a Tsunami of the Spirit to well up from within and crash down from above and overflow to the worlds in which God has deployed us all in this great salvation war.

Conversation Around Covenant

Rader and Rader

Commissioner Kay and General Paul Rader are participating in another book project that is scheduled to include this chapter. We've included it here for you to get a taste of their testimony and hear a bit of their hearts about their lives and callings.

General Paul A. Rader and Commissioner *Kay F. Rader in Conversation on Salvation Army Officership.* [30]

PAR: A lifetime of service certainly gives us a unique perspective on officership over the long haul.

KFR: Long, but never boring. How often have we said, we may die of something, but it won't be of boredom!

PAR: Is there any calling that is more diverse, colorful, fascinating, challenging and rewarding than officership? Not a walk in the park, sometimes intense and demanding, but always deeply rewarding.

KFR: What do you think has kept us at it all these years?

PAR: Bottom line: a sense of calling. The confidence that this is God's will for our lives. We have to admit that how that call is experienced is not the same for everyone.

KFR: Isaiah 30:21 tells us, "Your ears will hear a word behind you, 'This is the way, walk in it.'" I wish it could be that certain for everyone.

PAR: Psalm 32:8 has always been reassuring for me: "I will instruct you and teach you in the way you should go; I will counsel you with my loving eye on you." God has a way of opening a door and nudging us toward it by his Spirit.

KFR: Yes! Those who have ears to hear and hearts to obey want to respond as Isaiah did when he was touched with fire, "Here am I, send me!" However it comes, a settled sense that we are on the path of God's purpose as officers has taken us through the difficult points in the journey.

PAR: And there have been some testing times.

KFR: For one thing, we never knew where our response to God's call was going to take us. I love the plaque in our kitchen that pictures a little tent topped with an Army flag and says, "Home is where the Army sends me!" Along with all the positive and the Divine Yes that resonates in our hearts, we accept the disciplines of an Army— an Army of Salvation, an Army of peace, but nevertheless an Army. And that means being where ever we are needed in the line of battle.

PAR: Officership is not about contract. It is about covenant. It begins with our commitment to Jesus Christ and the reality of our relationship to him. It is grounded in our experience of his saving life. Our relationship to him is covenantal. And when we have responded to his call, our relationship to the Army is really not unlike the marriage covenant. Officers enter into a covenant relationship of trust and loyal commitment: each to the other, and both to God. The Army commits to provide for its officers as long as they are faithful to their calling. The Army depends on us and we depend on the Army. But there is no binding legal contract. It is all a matter of calling and covenant, mutual trust and commitment.

KFR: One of the great joys of officership for married couples is the privilege of working so closely together in a common calling. We have been able to work off of each other's strengths, supporting and encouraging one another. You remember that at our wedding, Dad Rader quoted this verse: "One shall chase a thousand and two shall put ten thousand to flight! As married officers we signed individual covenants, committing us to "live to win souls ... as the first great purpose of [our lives]... to be true to The Salvation Army, and the principles represented by its Flag." But the Army, after all, is about teamwork, an egalitarian partnership that crosses gender lines gently.

PAR: The covenant is not intended to be joint. It is a transaction that must occur between the individual and God. It is, however, signed and sealed with a common purpose that is shared by all officers, whether with one's spouse or a colleague officer with whom we may be teamed — all of this, is an accepted part of God's plan for our lives as officers in The Salvation Army.

KFR: Our covenant committed us to the holy mission of the Army. It has been expressed in many ways. The International Mission Statement is this:

> The Salvation Army, an international movement, is an evangelical part of the universal Christian Church. Its message is based on the Bible. Its ministries are motivated by love for god. Its mission is to preach the Gospel of Jesus Christ and meet human need in his name without discrimination.

Our calling and covenant commit us to the mission. Officership requires allegiance to the mission, under the lordship of Jesus Christ, believing in its principles and goals and methods and being fully comfortable with its ethos.

PAR: That is why full immersion in the training experience is so critical.

KFR: One of the most exciting dimensions of officership is the wide open door it provides for creativity and innovation in our service. There is such a rich diversity of ministry opportunities. And always fresh ways to address the needs of those we serve and with whom we share the Gospel.

PAR: For one thing, officership makes us part of a global missionary movement. It can provide a platform for service anywhere in the world. It puts us totally at God's disposal to send us where he will and use us as pleases him most.

KFR: Officership does not give us a blank sheet of paper and a packet of crayons and say draw whatever you want. But within the expectations and guidelines the Army affords — and the Army itself is part of a divinely creative process — there is unlimited scope for a lifetime of ministry as colorful and inventive as God by His Spirit can help us to make it.

PAR: We need to say something about officership being long-term. It is not a sprint. It's a marathon. O.K., that is a hard sell these days. Maybe, more than ever before. People tend to be into short-term commitments with all options open and unhampered control of one's life choices. Let's be honest. When God laid his hand hot upon us and claimed us by his grace for this ministry, it meant signing on for the duration.

KFR: Actually, the Soldier's Covenant (what we used to call, "The Articles of War") signed by every soldier, commits us to a lifetime covenant of service within the Army. It is part of the uniqueness of our movement that we expect that level of commitment from all our members. Officer covenants go deeper by extending this promise to exclude other employment outside the bounds of the Army until retirement, and an expectation that even after retirement, officers will give willing service as opportunities arise. This is long term.

In the early days of overseas missionary service, the candidate understood his/her covenant to be lifelong. British born Amy Carmichael, famous missionary to India, committed her life to the people of India for a lifetime, never returning home for furlough, living out her life, dying and being buried among the people of the Dohnavuhr Fellowship, which she founded. Elisabeth Elliott entitles her biography of this great saint, *A Chance to Die.*

PAR: Officership provides its own "chance to die" and "chance to live" for heaven's highest purpose: sharing the Gospel in its transforming power and living out the love of Christ for our lost and broken world. For "he died for all, that those who live should no longer live for themselves, but for him who died and was raised again" (2 Corinthians 5:14 TNIV). But let's be up front about the cost, because Jesus was. "Whoever wants to be my disciple," Jesus said, "must deny themselves and take up their cross daily and follow me. For whoever wants to save their life will lose it, but whoever loses their life for me will save it" (Luke 9:23, 24 TNIV).

KFR: Officership is long-term service: service to God and the Army for a life-time. Officership is not working for the Army. Officership is being the Army. Officership is belonging to an elite "company of the committed." The fellowship among the officers with whom we may be privileged to serve is beautiful.

PAR: What a privilege to wear the same uniform they wear. We have met them all over the world — many serving in hostile environments, in difficult and dangerous circumstances. The uniforms may differ but they are all identifiable as Army. When we meet these heroes and heroines, we know we share a common covenant and are engaged in the same great mission. The uniform itself is sacramental. Putting it on may be difficult, but as one Korean officer observed, "taking it off is more difficult."

KFR: Whatever the challenges, the rewards of this life are great beyond telling. And best of all is knowing that to follow Christ into officership in answer to His call is to bring joy to the heart of God. In the end, that is all that matters.

General Paul A. Rader (Ret.)
Commissioner Kay F. Rader
Lexington, Kentucky
July 2010

Author Resources

(Noland/Court)

Joe Noland
These are Joe's books:
Lean Right, Love Left: Balancing the Body
HOPE: A Flight Manual For Prospective Angels
A Little Greatness
No Limits Together: Vision Infinity
Booth Tucker and the Fringle
Out of the Rubble... Revolution!
(http://www.smashwords.com/books/view/14719)

Joe has produced these films:
Unsung 9/11
Altar's In The Street

Joe produced this CD:
Touch Through Me
You can connect with Joe's creativity at these websites:
www.joenoland.com
www.savn.tv
wwww.revolutionhawaii.com
Facebook: Joe Noland - Social Media Soldiers
Twitter: #joenoland
Linked In: Joe Noland

Stephen Court

Tweets at StephenCourt
Blogs at armybarmyblog.blogspot.ca
Edits Journal of Aggressive Christianity – armybarmy.com/jac.html

Has these books out:

Salvationism 101 with Danielle Strickland
Be a Hero with Wesley Campbell
Proverbial Leadership with Wesley Harris
Revolution with Aaron White
The Uprising with Olivia Munn
One Thing with Jim Knaggs
One Day with Jim Knaggs
One Army with Jim Knaggs
Hallmarks of the Salvation Army with Henry Gariepy
Holiness Incorporated with Geoff Webb and Rowan Castle
Boston Common (editor)
Greater Things with James Thompson
Army on its Knees with Janet Munn
High Counsel with Joe Noland
A Field for Exploits with Eva Burrows
Boundless with Danielle Strickland

Endnotes

STAGE 2

[1] Kevin Mannoia, *The Holiness Manifesto* (Grand Rapids: Wm. B. Eerdmans Publishing, 2008), 3-4.

[2] Ibid, 5.

[3] Harvey Cox, *Fire from Heaven: The Rise of Pentecostal Spirituality and the Reshaping of Religion in the Twenty-first Century* (Reading: Addison-Wesley, 1995) p. xv.

[4] Richard J. Foster, *Streams of Living Water: Celebrating the Great Traditions of Christian Faith* (San Francisco: Harper San Francisco, 1998) p. 25.

[5] Nathanael is also listed with the disciples in John 21:2.

[6] Notably, Nathanael is correct. Hebrews would know the Messiah was to emerge from Bethlehem not Nazareth. It is his generalization and obvious prejudice that are on display.

[7] Leon Morris, *The Gospel According to John.* Rev. ed. (Grand Rapids: Eerdmans, 1995), 358.

[8] Wesley, Sermon 43, "The Scripture Way of Salvation" in *The Works of John Wesley,* ed. Thomas Jackson, 14 vols., CD-ROM edition (Franklin: Providence House, 1994), 2: 158.

[9] Included in the Appendix are both William Booth and John Wesley's recommended examinations.

[10] The General of The Salvation Army, *The Salvation Army Handbook of Doctrine,* (London: Salvation Books, 2010), 321.

[11] Wesley, *Preface to Hymns and Sacred Poems* (1739) *Works.* (Jackson) 14:321.

[12] Albert Outler agrees that the linkage between sola fides and sanctification is unprecedented in Protestantism. While the Reformers recognized the linkage, Welsey accounted for a regenerative process between justification and sanctification. Outler, *Wesleyan Spirit,* 39.

[13] Howard Snyder, "What is Unique About a Wesleyan Theology of Mission?" accessed July 28, 2011, available from http://www.wineskins.net/pdf/wesleyan_mission.pdf

[14] John D. Michael Henderson, *Wesley's Class Meetings: a Model for Making Disciples,*

(Nappanee: Evangel Publishing House, 1997), 118-19.

[15] Asbury College Registrar's Annual Report 1938-1939, p. 62. Asbury University Archives.

[16] Henry C. James and Paul Rader, *Halls Aflame: An Account of the Spontaneous Revivals at Asbury College in 1950 and 1958*, Wilmore, Kentucky: The Department of Evangelism, Asbury Theological Seminary, 1966.

[17] *The War Cry*, November 19, 1988, p.14; Letter to author, Commissioner William E. Chamberlain, Atlanta, Georgia, Dec. 29, 1972; Major Mike Himes, "Asbury College: A Salvationist Alma Mater," *The War Cry*, March 29, 2008, pp. 11-14, repeated in *The Young Salvationist*, April 2008, pp. 6-9

[18] Asbury College Board of Trustees, Minutes of meetings of October 8-9, 1968 and April 8, 1969. Held in Office of the President, Asbury University. At the time Miller was director of public relations for the Greater New York Division.

[19] Paul Rader, Convocation Message, Fall 2004, in Asbury University Archives, File 214; Rader, "Salvation Army and Missiology," pp.8-9.

[20] Rader, Convocation Message 2004.

[21] Warren L. Maye, "'Laser-focused' learning: SA East, Asbury University form historic partnership," *Good News* (US Eastern Territorial newsletter) October 2013, p.1 and 3.

The author wishes especially to thank Mrs. Suzanne Gehring and Ms. Hannah Armour of the Asbury University Archives, Dr. Sandra Gray and Mrs. Dana Moutz of the President's Office and the staff of the Asbury University Registrar, for their invaluable assistance in preparing this paper.

STAGE 3

[1] Frances Ridley Havergal, *Song Book of The Salvation Army* (Verona, NJ: The Salvation Army, 1986), 612.

[2] Paul Evdokimov, quoted in Michael Plekon, *Hidden Holiness* (Notre Dame, IN: University of Notre Dame Press, 2009), 20.

[3] Samuel Logan Brengle, *Love Slaves* (Atlanta: The Salvation Army, 1923, 1982), 73.

[4] Quoted in Michael Plekon, vii.

[5] Quoted in Gordon Thomas, "Re-minting Christian Holiness," *The Officer*

[6] Emily Dickinson in Harold Bloom, *Best Poems of the English Language* (New York: Harper, 2004), 586

[7] Dag Hammarskjold, *Markings*, translated by Leif Sjoberg and W.H. Auden (New York: Knopf, 1965), 122.

[8] Andrew Bonar, *Robert Murray M'Cheyne* (London: Banner of Truth Trust, 1844), 159.

[9] Donald Burke, "Are We Biblically Illiterate?" *Salvationist* (August 2011), 18.

[10] Calvin Miller, *The Vanishing Evangelical: Saving the Church from Its Own Success by Restoring What Really Matters* (Grand Rapids: Baker, 2013), 29,107.

[11] Evelyn Underhill, *The Fruits of the Spirit* (London: Longmans, Green, 1942), 4.

[12] George McDonald, *Diary of an Old Soul* (Minneapolis: Augsburg), 43.

[13] Sister Vandana, *Waters of Fire* (Madras: Christian Literature Society, 1981), 11.

[14] *The Salvation Army Handbook of Doctrine* (London: Salvation Books, 2010), 299.

[15] Albert Orsborn, Song Book of The Salvation Army, 647.

[16] Norman Grubb, *The Law of Faith* (Fort Washington, PA: Christian Literature Crusade, 1947), 31.

[17] Paul Rader in John Merritt, ed., *Historical Dictionary of The Salvation Army* (Lanham, MD: Scarecrow, 2006), 136.

[18] Amy Carmichael in John Houghton, *Amy Carmichael of Dohnavur: The Story of a Lover and Her Beloved* (London: Hodder and Stoughton, 1953), 56.

[19] For example, see R. David Rightmire, *Sanctified Sanity: The Life and Teaching of Samuel Logan Brengle* (Alexandria, Virginia: The Salvation Army, 2003).

[20] Samuel L. Brengle, *Helps to Holiness* (London: Salvationist Publishing and Supplies, LTD, 1896. Reprinted 1955), pp. 130-135.

[21] Ibid., p. 130.

[22] Ibid., p. 131.

[23] Ibid., p. 133.

[24] Ibid., p. 135.

[25] Brengle's basic explanation of "waiting on God" can be found in his *Helps to Holiness*, p. 38-39.

[26] *Helps to Holiness*, p. 131.

[27] R. David Rightmire, *Sanctified Sanity*, pp. 126-127. For finding Brengle's basic explanation of the meaning of waiting on God, see his books *Helps to Holiness* (p. 38-39) and *At the Center of the Circle: Selections from Published and Unpublished Writings of Samuel Logan Brengle* (John D. Waldron. ed., [Kansas City: Beacon Hill, 1976], pp. 13-14).

[28] For basic understanding of Brengle's doctrinal concept of the Wesleyan synergism, see his book *The Way of Holiness* (Atlanta, Georgia: The Salvation Army Supplies and Purchasing Dept., 1949), pp. 15-16. It is crucial to correctly understand that Brengle's theological position on this subject should not be confused with the heretic beliefs of Pelagianism or semi-Pelagianism. Unfortunately, Glen O'Brien impatiently misrepresents Brengle's soteriological writings on Wesleyan synergism by introducing Pelagian or semi-Pelagian thought in his article "Why Brengle? Why Coutts? Why Not?" *(Word & Deed*, Vol. 13, No. 1. November 2010, p. 9).

[29] *Helps to Holiness*, p. 134. Considering the synergic nature of waiting on God, Brengle also asserted that "we must stir up the gift of prayer that is within us, we must exercise ourselves in prayer until our souls sweat, and then we shall realize the mighty energy of the Holy Ghost interceding within us" *(Helps to Holiness*, p, 134).

[30] David Rightmire, *Sanctified Sanity*, p. 126.

[31] Samuel L. Brengle, *Love-Slaves* (Atlanta, Georgia: The Salvation Army Supplies and Purchasing Dept., 1960), p. 78.

[32] *The new Salvation Army Handbook of Doctrine* (2010) briefly describes the rubric of the Wesleyan way of salvation as follows: "Wesley saw holiness as being a part of the complete way of salvation, the *via salutis* which begins with regeneration, the new birth which accompanies justification. From that instantaneous work it increases gradually until there is another work in which cleansing from sin results in a heart of 'perfect love', by which Wesley meant purity of motivation or intent, a sincerity of love. The sanctifying process then continues until its completion at the believer's death or glorification." *(The Salvation Army Handbook of Doctrine*, [London, UK: The Salvation Army International Headquarters, 2010], p. 213).

[33] *Helps to Holiness*, p. 130.

[34] For Wesley, prevenient grace is God's initial restoring grace that comes before conversion in relation to fallen humanity. Wesley saw that prevenient grace brings the first stage of awakening the spiritual sense towards God, and it opens up the possibility of genuine knowledge of God in "some degree of salvation."

[35] Kenneth J. Collins, *The Theology of John Wesley: Holy Love and the Shape of Grace* (Nashville: Abingdon Press, 2007), pp. 80-82.

[36] William R. Cannon, *The Theology of John Wesley: With Special Reference to the Doctrine of Justification* (Nashville: Abingdon-Cokesbury Press, 1946), pp. 107-108. Robert E. Chiles, *Theological Transition in American Methodism: 1790-1935* (New York: University Press of America, 1965. Reprinted 1983), p.149. Jason E. Vickers, "Wesley's theological emphases" in Randy L. Maddox and Jason E. Vickers, eds. *The Cambridge Companion to John Wesley* (New York: Cambridge University Press, 2010), p. 201.

[37] Kenneth J. Collins, *The Theology of John Wesley*, p. 80.

[38] *Helps to Holiness*, p. 132.

[39] Ibid., p. 132.

[40] Ibid., p. 132.

[41] Young Sung Kim, "Tongsung Kido" in *Journal of Aggressive Christianity*, Issue 84, April-May 2013. http://www.armybarmy.com/pdf/JAC_Issue_084.pdf

[42] Carroll Ferguson Hunt, *If Two Shall Agree: The Story of Paul A. Rader and Kay F. Rader of The Salvation Army* (Kansas City, Missouri: Beacon Hill Press of Kansas City, 2001), p. 44-116.

[43] *The Way of Holiness*, p. 84.

STAGE 4

[1] The title and heading quotes from this chapter are from the Raders' joint McPherson Lecture in Australia Southern Territory, August 2010, called Transformations. http://armybarmy.com/pdf/JAC_Issue_070.pdf

[2] The popular number is 80,000 but of course it is very difficult to nail.

[3] http://www.ted.com/talks/bono_the_good_news_on_poverty_yes_there_s_good_news.html

[4] Nestle, Cadbury. Mars, Verkade, Swiss Noir and others have gone or are going fair trade.

[5] Reports of dead people coming back to life, for example, as in "Dead-Raising," 2012. Journal of Aggressive Christianity. *www.armybarmy.com/pdf/JAC_Issue_082.pdf*

[6] And the Multiplication Mandate of 2 Timothy 2:2 presents a contagious discipleship as the means of fulfilling our mission.

[7] Christianity in its Global Context, 2013. P7. http://wwwgordonconwell.com/netcommunity/CSGCResources/ChristianityinitsGlobalContext.pdf

[8] According to Operation World, as report in same source, p17. http://wwwgordonconwell.com/netcommunity/CSGCResources/ChristianityinitsGlobalContext.pdf

[9] The largest Salvation Army American Territory is USA Eastern, with 363 corps – according to "2013 Territorial Comparisons" document.

[10] Charisma Magazine August 2013 cover story ASSEMBLIES 2.0.

[11] "Divine order: God goes super on our natural" – 1 Corinthians 15:46 Boundless New Testament. The pertinent endnote from BNT 1 Corinthians 15:46: all = otherwise, on the other hand; + epeita = thereafter (implies divine order, thus "divine order," and natural is followed by supernatural, so "God wants to go super on your natural"); pneumatikon = spiritual (super); psuchikon = natural (natural). hat tip Peter Mitchell).

[12] The Salvation Army faces a danger, with influential forces within, even today, wanting to remove "salvation" and "army" from our name and character, leaving us with the inoffensive, tolerance-saturated, impotent but pervasively-acceptable appellation… how about The Helping Group?

[13] Boundless New Testament. Footnotes on that rendition of those verses: huper = over, exceeding, abundantly, + huper (!) = over, exceeding, abundantly, + perissos = superabundantly (boundless… exceeds); dunamis = force (force); aiteo = ask, crave, desire, require (crave); noeo = perceive, understand, think upon, heed, ponder, consider (perceive); energeo = active, efficient… be mighty in (active); dunamis (again) = force (dynamically) ["active" verb tense present middle participle] ekklesia = a calling out, an assembly ("the called out"); doxa = praise, glory (magnify); pasa = all, every (every); geneas = race, family, generation (nation, from "race"); aionos = space of time, age, + ainon = space of time, age (this and every generation)

[14] This source explains that Moody was applying a statement by revivalist Henry Varley to himself - http://www.christianitytoday.com/ch/1990/issue25/2510.html

[15] We are lifting this from the Raders' joint McPherson Lecture in Australia Southern Territory, August 2010, called Transformations. http://armybarmy.com/pdf/JAC_Issue_070.pdf

[16] http://www.cbeinternational.org/?q=content/our-mission-and-history

[17] "Men, Women and Biblical Equality"
http://www.cbeinternational.org/?q=content/men-women-and-biblical-equality

[18] http://sojo.net/blogs/2009/10/06/jesus-didnt-overlook-gender-he-transcended-it

[19] Gordon D. Fee, *Listening to the Spirit in the Text* (Grand Rapids, MI: Eerdmans, 2000), 56.

[20] Christine Parkin, "A Woman's Place," in *Catherine Booth, Her Continuing Relevance,* Clifford Kews, ed., (St. Albans, VT: The Campfield Press, 1990) 11-12.

[21] William Booth. *Messages to Soldiers* (London; The Salvation Army, 1908) referenced on the Salvation Army international website, www.salvationarmy.org.

[22] Diane Winston, *Red Hot and Righteous: The Urban Religion of the Salvation Army.* (Cambridge, MA: Harvard University Press, 1999) 95.

[23] Andrew Mark Eason, *Women in God's Army: Gender and Equality in the Early Salvation Army* (Waterloo, Ontario: Wilfrid Laurier University Press, 2003) 157.

[24] Carroll Ferguson Hunt, *If Two Shall Agree.* (Kansas City, MS: Beacon Hill Press, 2001) 150.

[25] Kay Rader, "Keeping the Dream Alive," in *Terms of Empowerment: Salvation Army Women in Ministry* (The Salvation Army USA Eastern Territory, West Nyack, NY: 2001, 79.

[26] Hunt, 167.

[27] Ibid.

[28] Paul A. Rader, "Partners in Mission," The War Cry (USA) July 24, 1999, 11.

[29] As you will expect in any Salvationist production, the appeal.

[30] Excerpt from the forthcoming book, CHARGE! By Joe Noland and Stephen Court.

CREST BOOKS

Salvation Army National Publications

Crest Books, a division of The Salvation Army's National Publications department, was established in 1997 so contemporary Salvationist voices could be captured and bound in enduring form for future generations, to serve as witnesses to the continuing force and mission of the Army.

Stephen Banfield and Donna Leedom, *Say Something*

Judith L. Brown and Christine Poff, eds., *No Longer Missing: Compelling True Stories from The Salvation Army's Missing Persons Ministry*

Terry Camsey, *Slightly Off Center! Growth Principles to Thaw Frozen Paradigms*

Marlene Chase, *Pictures from the Word; Beside Still Waters: Great Prayers of the Bible for Today; Our God Comes: And Will Not Be Silent*

John Cheydleur and Ed Forster, eds., *Every Sober Day Is a Miracle*

Helen Clifton, *From Her Heart: Selections from the Preaching and Teaching of Helen Clifton*

Shaw Clifton, *Never the Same Again: Encouragement for New and Not–So–New Christians; Who Are These Salvationists? An Analysis for the 21st Century; Selected Writings, Vol. 1: 1974-1999 and Vol. 2: 2000-2010*

Christmas Through the Years: A War Cry Treasury

Frank Duracher, *Smoky Mountain High*

Easter Through the Years: A War Cry Treasury

Ken Elliott, *The Girl Who Invaded America: The Odyssey Of Eliza Shirley*

Ed Forster, *101 Everyday Sayings From the Bible*

William Francis, *Celebrate the Feasts of the Lord: The Christian Heritage of the Sacred Jewish Festivals*

Henry Gariepy, *Israel L. Gaither: Man with a Mission; A Salvationist Treasury: 365 Devotional Meditations from the Classics to the Contemporary; Andy Miller: A Legend and a Legacy*

Henry Gariepy and Stephen Court, *Hallmarks of The Salvation Army*

Roger J. Green, *The Life & Ministry of William Booth* (with Abingdon Press, Nashville)

How I Met The Salvation Army

Carroll Ferguson Hunt, *If Two Shall Agree* (with Beacon Hill Press, Kansas City)

John C. Izzard, *Pen of Flame: The Life and Poetry of Catherine Baird*

David Laeger, *Shadow and Substance: The Tabernacle of the Human Heart*

John Larsson, *Saying Yes to Life, Inside a High Council*

Living Portraits Speaking Still: A Collection of Bible Studies

Herbert Luhn, *Holy Living: The Mindset of Jesus*

Philip Needham, *He Who Laughed First: Delighting in a Holy God,* (with Beacon Hill Press, Kansas City); *When God Becomes Small*

R.G. Moyles, *I Knew William Booth; Come Join Our Army; William Booth in America: Six Visits 1886 - 1907; Farewell to the Founder*

Joe Noland, *A Little Greatness*

Quotes of the Past & Present

Lyell M. Rader, *Romance & Dynamite: Essays on Science & the Nature of Faith*
R. David Rightmire, *Sanctified Sanity: The Life and Teaching of Samuel Logan Brengle*

Allen Satterlee, *Turning Points: How The Salvation Army Found a Different Path; Determined to Conquer: The History of The Salvation Army Caribbean Territory; In the Balance: Christ Weighs the Hearts of 7 Churches*

Harry Williams, *An Army Needs An Ambulance Corps: A History of The Salvation Army's Medical Services*

A. Kenneth Wilson, *Fractured Parables: And Other Tales to Lighten the Heart and Quicken the Spirit; The First Dysfunctional Family: A Modern Guide to the Book of Genesis, It Seemed Like a Good Idea at the Time: Some of the Best and Worst Decisions in the Bible*

A Word in Season: A Collection of Short Stories

Check Yee, *Good Morning China*

Chick Yuill, *Leadership on the Axis of Change*